1

BookCasters

An Author's Guide to Writing a Bestselling Book

This document may be used independently or as a Companion Guide to **BookCasters'** Webinars with Media Queens Julie and Nicki.

By Julie Lokun, JD

&

Nicki Pascarella

THE
MEDIACASTERS
PUBLISHING

©2022

CROWN AND COMPASS | Linktree

Having been asked many times in my career, I can tell you my strategy for successfully writing three best-selling books. Hint: I didn't do it alone.

From ideas, testing my material, developing the book, to marketing strategies, writing a book has many phases to the process. For all three of my books, I created support groups that helped me along the way (as I helped them with their projects). These support teams met weekly and kept the process moving.

I hear a quote in my head from Barbara Sher, author of *Teamworks!* "People have more courage you for than you have for yourself."

Who do you know in your life that could be part of your team? Who do you know that is working on big goals and projects? Be the leader, start a team and get the courage and inspiration to work on your book…from idea to marketing.

Bookcaster's: An Author's Guide to Writing A Bestselling Book will give you the clarity you need for all the steps and processes.

Start with this guide, enroll some friends in goal-setting adventures and plan your future book signing.

Michael J. Losier
Author of *Law of Attraction*, *Law of Connection*, and *Your Life's Purpose*

Dear Reader,

Welcome to the first step in becoming a published author. We know you have a best-selling book in you that is just itching to be published. We understand this calling to put pen to paper. This constant nudge that tickles your brain and envelopes your heart is a space where so many writers get stuck. The task of writing a book, publishing a book, and then marketing your book can seem like an overwhelming summit to climb. This is the reason Nicki Pascarella and I, Julie Lokun, put together this comprehensive guide to help you on your writing and publishing journey.

I have been writing for as long as I can remember. I basked in the glory of seeing my readers (who were at the time my mom, dad, and grandmother) delight in my prose. I rose to glory as my High School Newspaper's editor and promptly applied to the prestigious Ernie Pyle School of Journalism at Indiana University.

Then it all stopped. My writing stopped. My unique perspective on the world was muted. I became distracted with life. I became disenchanted with the $10 per hour wage journalists were offered, and my life marched on. Not until I entered my forties, and my children could manage basic life-sustaining tasks did I start to dabble in the creative arts. My passion was quickly reignited, and I began to write—and write. I blogged, I wrote articles, and I wrote books. When my fairy-godmother, Nicki Pascarella, entered my life, I knew I was meant to do something more with writing. I knew I was meant to empower the voices of the marginalized, and the dismissed authors who were overlooked by publishing house conglomerates. Nicki whispered into my ear, "You should start your own publishing company." This publishing company would be like no other. It would be mission-driven and be a source of inspiration, education, and fascination. Thus, *MediaCasters Publishing* was born.

This guide will give you a glimpse into our blood, sweat, and tears. This guide will equip you to write, brand, publish and market your best-seller. Each page will elicit confidence in knowing that you are on your way to unleashing your literary genius onto the world. Sharpen your pencils and carve out space to commit to your writing. Then, just do it.

You've got this!

Jules

The Dragonfly symbolizes change and growth in mental and emotional maturity, as well as understanding the deeper meaning of life.

CONTENTS

Every book starts with a spark of creativity! Let's get that fire burning.

"The desire to create is one of the deepest yearnings of the human soul."

-Dieter F. Uchtdorf

ON BEING AN ARTIST

Let's start by exploring Joseph Beuy's quote, *"Every Human being is an artist."* With this profound quote also comes the theory that art, in all forms, is a catalyst for bringing your book to life.

Why?

1. Art improves creativity.

2. Art gives you joy.

3. Art relieves stress.

"Art washes away from the soul the dust of everyday life." Pablo Picasso

What does this mean? Be sure to stop and smell the roses and enjoy the art that others create so that you can bring your project to fruition.

Tip-Let the art that others create inspire your creativity.

Abraham Maslow, a humanistic psychologist, described self-actualization as the process of becoming *"everything you are capable of becoming."* Maslow's Hierarchy states that human beings require certain needs to be met. This includes the areas of physiological, safety, love, esteem, and self-actualization. Let's examine the highest need, self-actualization.

Creativity is one of the most important aspects of becoming self-actualized.

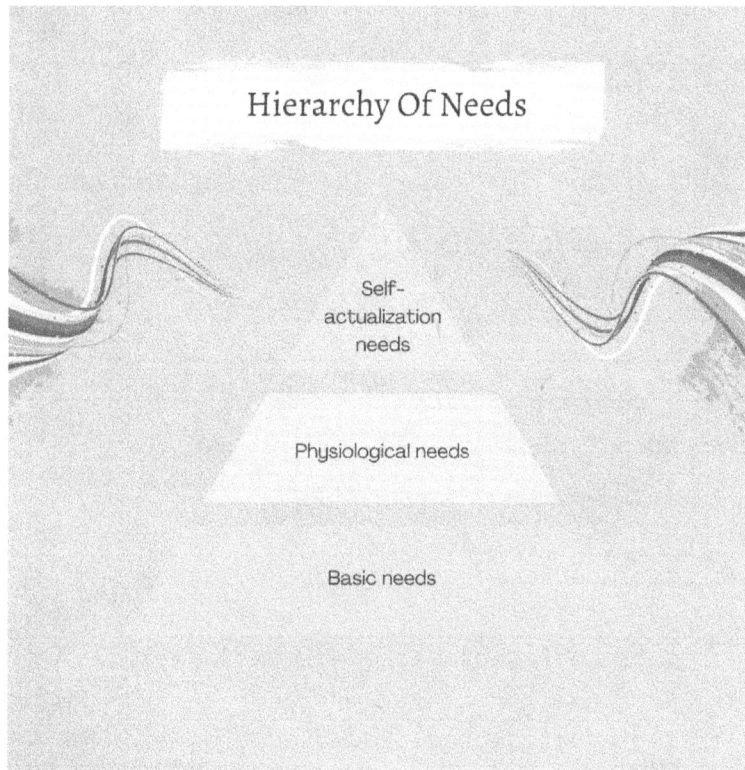

Hierarchy Of Needs

Self-actualization needs

Physiological needs

Basic needs

"We all need to express ourselves. We have the need to create our world, ourselves, and our dreams. The need to experience safety, love, esteem, and wellbeing is to experience our true nature of abundance and divinity. As creators, we need to create because that's what we are. The creative urge is the primary force of life. It is what created the physical universe and the purpose for our living." From www.mindreality

Do you think you are self-actualized? Yes/No? Why or why not?

_____

_____

If not, what can you do to change this?

_____

_____

> *"Creativity is the natural order of life. Life is energy: pure creative energy."* Julie Cameron

---

Fun Fact-Did you know that people who engage in handcrafts live longer?

What does creativity mean to you?

_____

_____

_____

What are your creative outlets?

1._____

2._____

3._____

List others here:

_____

_____

_____

Do you experience roadblocks in your creative pursuits?

_____

What are they?

_____

_____

_____

_____

What methods do you use to overcome these roadblocks? Think and Discuss:

_____

_____

_____

> *"So, you see, imagination needs moodling— long inefficient, happy idling, dawdling, and puttering."* Brenda Ueland

Fun Fact- A 2017 study in the journal PLOS ONE found that listening to "happy" music— defined as classical tunes that were upbeat and stimulating helped people to perform better on tasks that involved "divergent" thinking, which is a core component of creativity.

ON BECOMING CREATIVE

Try the following:

1. Make a weekly date with yourself to experience something new. Go to a museum. See a play. Read a book from a different genre. Take a painting or cooking class. Your imagination is your only limit.

2. Take ten minutes (or longer) each day to write in a journal. Use it as a brain dump. Write down whatever you are thinking. Once you clear your mind, creativity abounds.

3. Get in touch with Mother Nature. Take a walk, hike, or just throw a blanket under a tree and sit and meditate.

4. Listen to music. Classical music has been shown to increase dopamine which can reduce stress and help you feel more relaxed, lowering blood pressure. Try classical music. If it doesn't float your boat, listen to whatever you like. Put on a piece of music and just move—dance, sway, hop! Do whatever grabs you.

5. Give yourself permission to create without judgment. Create for joy!

6. Set small attainable goals.

7.Show up!

8. Create a positive mantra. Nicki's is, "I am a writer who dances beautifully."

Workspace to create a mantra

_____

_____

_____

MAKE A CREATIVE DATE

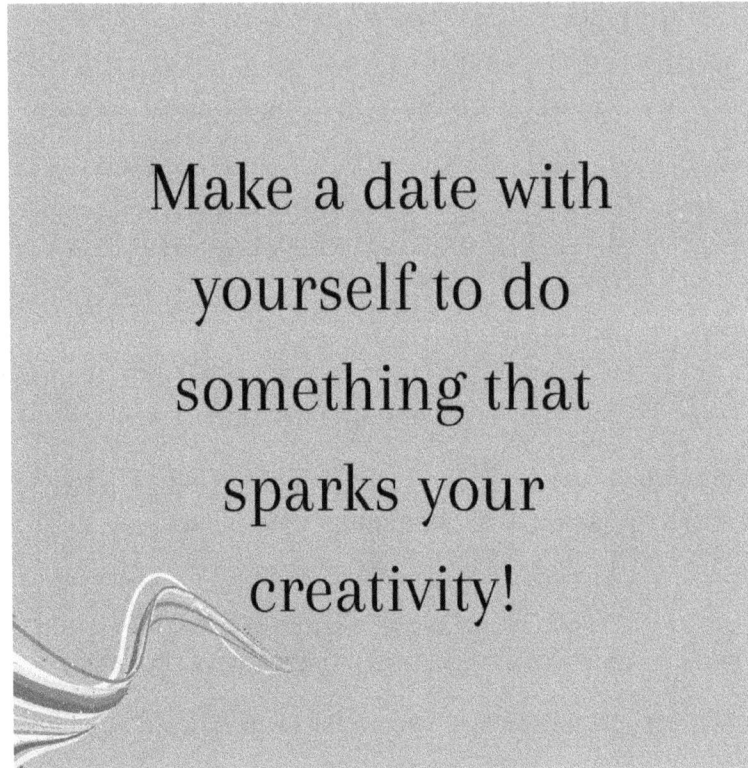

Make a date with yourself to do something that sparks your creativity!

It is important to spend introspective time to nurse your creative juices. As busy as life can get, it is imperative you set aside time to be inspired. Art in general feeds your soul.

Feeling uninspired, try one of the following:

Make a Creative Date

Go to a movie
See a play or musical
Read a book in a different genre
Sit under a tree and meditate
Take a walk
Try a new recipe
Write a poem
Set up an easel and paint a picture
Make a new vision board
Go to a museum
Listen to music
Go to a concert
Window shop at the craft store
Take a pottery class
Plan an afternoon hike
Experiment with a new photo app and make a fun
movie of family photos

The possibilities are endless. What would inspire your creativity?

Plan a month of creative dates.

1.

2.

3.

4.

Your Thoughts About Creativity. Think and Discuss:

_____
_____
_____
_____
_____
_____

Fun Fact-Listening to music relaxes the brain's focus while still allowing it to incubate new ideas. According to Markham Heid, there's evidence that listening to music can stimulate the brain's default mode network, which is a collection of connected brain regions that research has linked to creative insight.

Musical Creativity Activity:

1. Choose two pieces of music that are very different.

2. Listen to the first piece and draw whatever comes to mind.

3. Listen to the second piece and draw whatever comes to mind.

4. After listening to the two musical selections, think about how you felt. Was there one that seemed to help your creativity? How are your two pictures different? Think, write or Discuss?

Listen to the first piece of music and draw.

Listen to the second piece of music and draw.

Analyze your drawings and how the music made you feel.

_____
_____
_____
_____
_____
_____
_____
_____
_____

Every child is an artist. The problem is how to remain an artist once we grow up. Inspiration does exist, but it must find you working. Pablo Picasso.

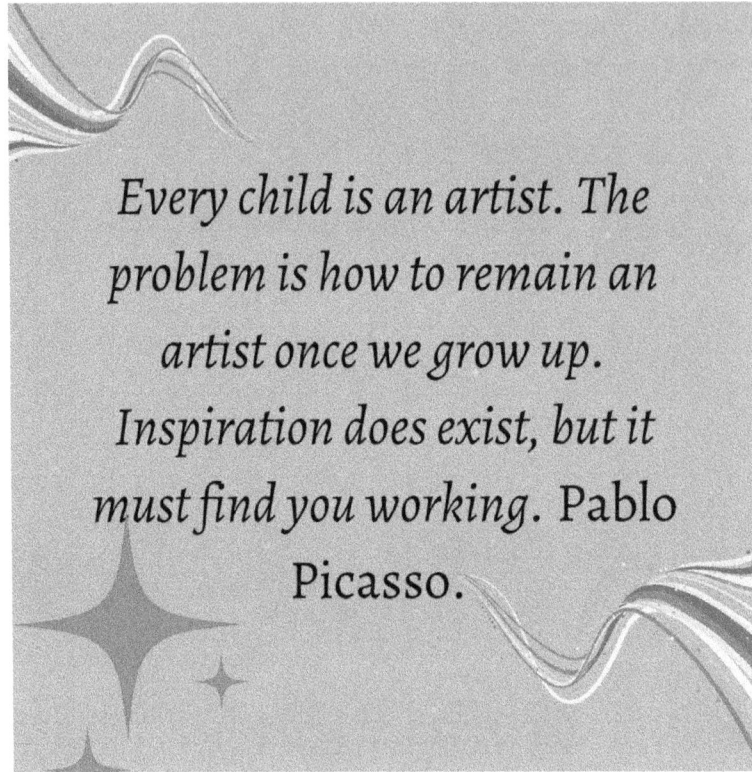

Journaling Activity:

1. Find a quiet place to sit and reflect.

2. List a few topics that are interesting/important to you.

    *   _____

    *   _____

    *   _____

    *   _____

    *   _____

3. Set a timer for ten minutes and just write about these topics. When you run out of things to say about one, write about the other. This is a No Judgement Zone!

_____

_____

_____

_____

_____

_____

_____

_____

Humans are storytellers and have been so since the beginning of time. Think of oral storytelling going back to the time of Beowulf. How about songs and poetry? Egyptian Hieroglyphics, caveman drawings, pictures on quilts, and braids on slaves are all examples of storytelling. Then there are movies, plays, and television shows.

Can you think of any other methods that mankind has used to tell stories?

_____

_____

Storytelling is the greatest technology that humans have ever created." Jon Westenberg

Tips for great Storytelling:

1. Self-knowledge and awareness are at the heart of every great story.

2. Every great story has a clear structure and purpose.

3. Great stories have a character people root for.

4. Great stories appeal to one of our six basic emotions—anger, disgust, fear, happiness, sadness, or surprise.

5. Great stories are surprising, unexpected, focused, and simple.

WHY WRITE?

1. Writing helps you think and assists the human mind in achieving its full potential. It allows people to make abstract ideas concrete.

2. Writing can help you feel good. James Pennebaker, a cognitive psychologist at the University of Texas-Austin, investigated the benefits of writing. He concluded writing helped heal emotional wounds and that short-term focused writing benefited those dealing with a terminal illness, victims of violent crimes, and new college students struggling with the transition from high school.

3. Writing gets important messages to people.

4. Writing allows individuals to educate and entertain.

5. Writing is empowering.

6. Writing helps you discover who you are.

7. Writing allows you to have an impact on others.

8. Writing allows you to create and become self-actualized.

Can you think of any other reasons you should write? List them below.

_____
_____
_____

COMBATING WRITER'S BLOCK
Why Aren't You Writing?

_____
_____
_____
_____
_____
_____

The following list can help you combat writer's block.

1. Allow yourself to be messy when you are creating. You can clean and perfect later.

2. Set aside time each day to write. Set a timer for five minutes to start. Increase it until you are able to write for thirty minutes at a time.

3. If you are experiencing writer's block, take a walk. Stretch. Mediate. Do yoga. Listen to music. Be gentle with yourself.

4. Have confidence in yourself. Know that you have the answer.

5. Don't forget to set a creative date with yourself.

TIME MANAGEMENT
Many authors list "*finding time to write*" as their number one problem. The Pomodoro Technique can help with this.

THE NUTS AND BOLTS—AND TOMATOES—OF THE POMODORO TECHNIQUE.
The Pomodoro Technique is a time management method developed by Francesco Cirillo that alternates timed work sessions with short breaks. The system promotes concentration and prevents mental fatigue. Cirillo used a timer to break work into 25-minute intervals. A short break separates each interval. Since Cirillo used a tomato-shaped kitchen timer to keep track of the intervals, he named them after the Italian word for tomato.

The system typically uses a 25-minute work session followed by a 5-minute break.

> ### How to Utilize the Pomodoro Technique
> 1. *Make your to-do list and grab a timer.*
> 2. *Set your timer for 25 minutes, then focus on a single task until the timer rings.*
> 3. *When your session ends, mark off one Pomodoro and record what you completed.*
> 4. *Take a five-minute break.*
> 5. *After four Pomodoros, take a 15-30 minute break.*

Experiment to find the time intervals that work best for you. Nicki finds the twenty-minute interval to be her sweet spot. Perhaps a thirty-minute work, ten-minute rest interval will fit your needs. Maybe a fifteen-minute work interval, 4-minute rest interval will be what you find most productive.

Start with twenty-five to five intervals and adjust until you find your sweet spot.

Nicki sets the timer on her phone for 20 minutes then focuses until the time is up. When her timer goes off, she takes a 6-minute break. She gets a drink of water, stretches, pats her dogs, uses the restroom, then gets back to it.

COMBATING CREATIVITY BLOCKS USING THE POMODORO TECHNIQUE

You can also use these time segments to work through writing and creativity blocks. Even if you have no idea what to write about, sit for twenty minutes and fill your blank page with words, phrases, and whatever else comes to mind.

Wa-lah! Three Pomodoros later, you have worked through your block The great thing is you can adapt this technique to any task.

If you want to write novels but work a full-time job and have limited time, set that timer once a day so that you aren't stagnating. Eventually, when life allows you a bit more time to focus on your project, you won't have a blank page staring at you.

Make this technique work for you. Don't fret if you only have ten minutes a day to devote to a task. The key is setting that timer, focusing, and getting it done!

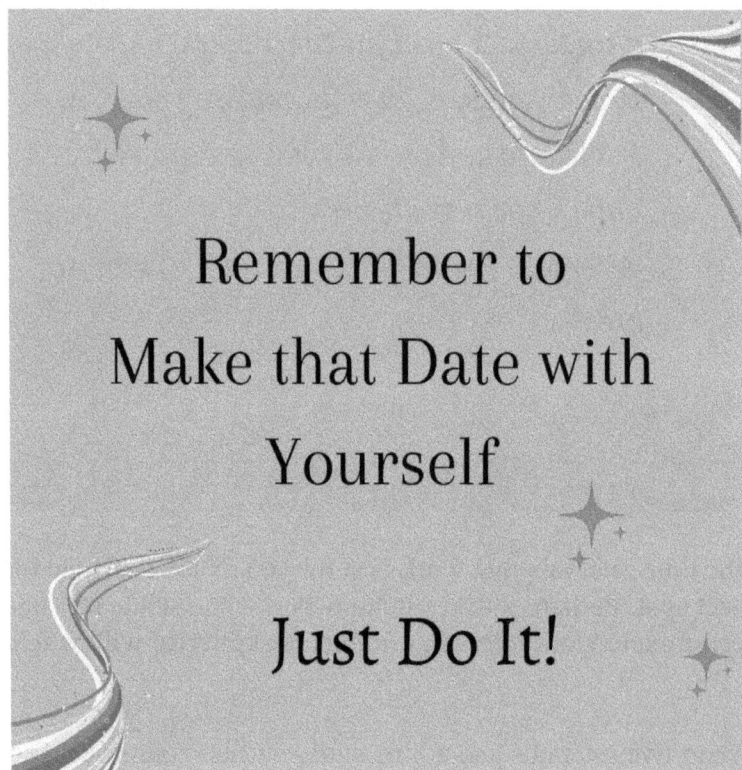

Remember to
Make that Date with
Yourself

Just Do It!

PLANNING YOUR BOOK

Are you a planner or a pantser?

A planner organizes the entire story outlining every plot point. A pantser flies by the seat of their pants and makes up the story as they go. Most people are a combination. Nicki tends to take notes before she starts writing, filling in the growth she wants to see in each of her characters, major plot points, and where the story needs to be in the end. Then she lets the minor details come to her as she writes.

Nicki's Writing Process in Googledocs

1. Starts with an overall idea of a character and a story.

2. Outlines major characters, plot, and ending.

3. Writes the first chapter in first and third person to see which voice fits her story.

4. After she chooses her POV, she starts her main document by adding her first chapter. She highlights the notes for the first chapter in her outline.

5. Writes the second chapter in a separate document in short twenty minutes segments. She does multiple sessions a day. Once the second chapter is done, she copies and pastes it into the main document. Then she highlights this section in the outline.

6. It is time to start chapter three. She repeats step 5 with each chapter until the first draft of the book is finished.

7. First Edit-She reads the book in a few settings (the less the better) to look for plot errors, readability, and overall feeling.

8. She makes a copy because she is getting ready to cut and paste.

9. Second Edit-She takes each chapter from the document, one at a time, performing a line edit. This is where she perfects every single sentence and word. Once the chapter is finished, she adds it back into the main document.

10. Third Edit-She puts the book away for at least a month and then pulls it out to do another edit. This time she leaves the document in one piece.

11. She sends the document to beta readers to get advice.

12. Fourth Edit-She edits with advice from the beta readers and is now ready to send out for a professional edit.

13. Fifth Edit-She takes the advice from the professional editor and does a final edit before sending to agents and publishers.

Tip-You must come up with your own process. Then you must constantly adapt it to fit your needs. Nicki's process works for her; it may not work for you.

YOUR WRITING PROCESS:
What do you think your first steps should be? Come back to this from time to time. Cross things out. Change things up. Soon you will have a process that allows you to find success.

Step 1

_____

_____

Step 2

_____

_____

Step 3

_____

_____

Step 4

_____

_____

Step 5

_____

_____

Step 6

_____

_____

Step 7

_____

_____

Step 8

_____

_____

Step 9

_____

_____

Step 10

_____

_____

Notes:

_____

_____

_____

_____

_____

_____

Complete the brainstorming below to prepare your masterpiece.

What **Genre** are you writing?
Who is your **Audience**?
What is your **Purpose?**   Will your audience laugh, be held in suspense, etc.?
What **Point of View** will you use?
What is your approximate **Word Count?**
Who are your **Main Characters** and **Secondary Characters?**   See the character development worksheet below.
World Building: Think Setting. Time, Place, Conditions

Sketch out your world below. Better yet, make a vision board, bulletin board, or collage of your world.

What **Narrative Style** will you use?
Descriptive narrative, Viewpoint narrative, Historical narrative, Linear narrative, Non-linear narrative

What is your **Theme?**
You can have more than one theme.

Tip: Read at least fifty books in your chosen genre.

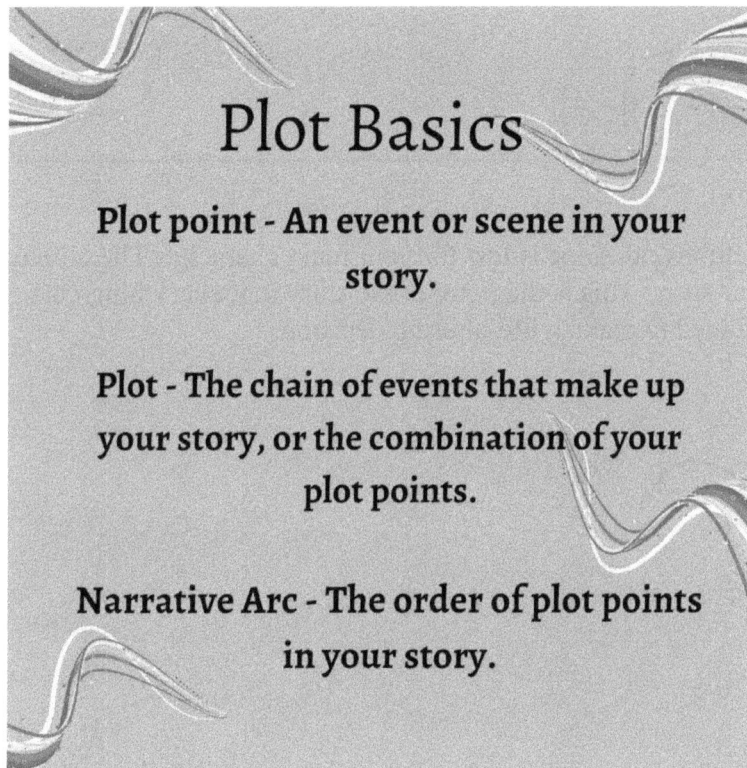

Plot Basics

Plot point - An event or scene in your story.

Plot - The chain of events that make up your story, or the combination of your plot points.

Narrative Arc - The order of plot points in your story.

PLOT

The 5 elements of Plot.

Use the chart below to make some notes on how you will achieve each element of plot.

Plot Point 1: Exposition

This only lasts a few chapters. Introduce your characters, establish the setting, and introduce the primary conflict of your story. Immediately place the reader in the action. What is your hook?

Plot Point 2: Rising Action and Inciting Incident

What is your inciting incident, or the moment that sets your story into action? Create tension as your conflict progresses. This will take up the largest chunk of your book.

Plot Point 3: Climax

Right before your climax, all hope is lost for your main character. The climax is the most exciting part of your story. This is the point in the story that everything changes, or where your main character is forced to make a life-altering decision.

Plot Point 4: Falling Action

Move toward that satisfying conclusion. Resolve the conflicts and subplots.

Plot Point 5. Resolution

Tie up the loose ends and bring your story to its happy or tragic ending.

Tip: Keep story ideas on index cards and come back to them when you are ready.

CHARACTERS

While fabulous plots mean exciting twists and turns, great character development is what draws readers in and makes them fall in love with your book. Here are some character development tools to assist you in creating fascinating characters.

Book Title
Character's Name

Physical Description:	Notes
Back Story:	
Goals:	
Motivation:	
Quirks	

Values	
Family/Friends	
Nemesis	

More Character notes

SHOW DON'T TELL

One of the biggest mistakes that new authors make is that they tell instead of show.

Telling means that you tell your readers what to think instead of letting them think for themselves. It is similar to giving them a secondhand report following the event that summarizes plot and distances the reader from the action.

Showing means you provide the reader with concrete vivid details, and they draw their own conclusions. It allows the reader to experience the events firsthand through the characters five senses. It involves the reader in the story and allows them to be an active participant.

This is one of the most difficult writing techniques to master. It is what takes authors from being amateur to best sellers. Entire books have been written on this concept. Be sure to comb your manuscript for places that you can provide more vivid descriptions and involve your reader in the action. Watch for those pesky passive verbs.

Tip: Check out Sandra Girth's free book on Amazon, *Show Don't Tell*.

Example:

Telling: Lisa was excited.

Showing: Lisa leaped from her chair and clapped. "Holy guacamole! I can't wait."

Now you try: Rewrite the sentence Lisa was excited three different ways, showing instead of telling.

1._____

_____

2._____

_____

3._____

_____

THE QUICK GUIDE TO WRITING NON-FICTION

Non-fiction is prose writing based on facts, real events, and real people, such as biographies and historical texts. This includes news stories, essays, documentaries, encyclopedias, and textbooks. The author's main purpose is to inform or educate readers on a certain topic.

BRAINSTORMING YOUR NON-FICTION PROJECT

Define your purpose for writing this book?
Why are you the person to tell this story? What makes you an expert?

What research will you use? Case studies, journals, interviews, your own experiences? Be sure you have your facts correct and use reputable sources.
What style will you use? Narrative, expository, persuasive, or descriptive?

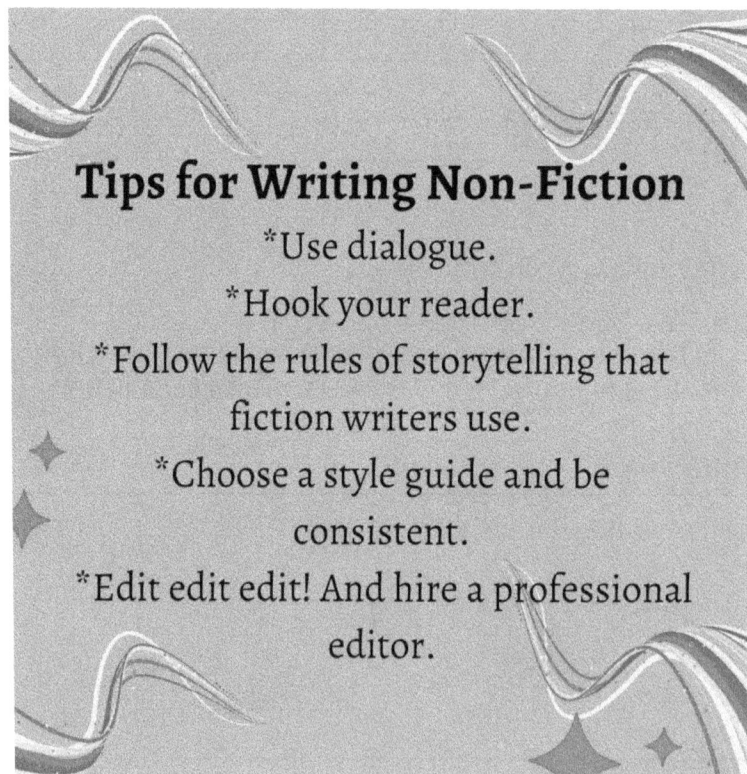

Tips for Writing Non-Fiction

*Use dialogue.

*Hook your reader.

*Follow the rules of storytelling that fiction writers use.

*Choose a style guide and be consistent.

*Edit edit edit! And hire a professional editor.

THE STYLES OF NON-FICTION WRITING.

Narrative Writing-Tells a true story about a person, event, or place. It can be written in first person and always involves research.

Expository Writing-Explains or informs a reader about a specific topic.

Persuasive Writing-Takes a position on an issue and argues for or against an opposing side. Uses facts and information to support the argument while influencing the readers' opinions. It can take the form of an op-ed piece or editorial in the newspaper.

Descriptive Writing-Employs the five senses to help the reader get a visual. Uses sensory language, rich details, and figurative language.

THE AVERAGE LENGTH OF BOOKS

Tip- The average fiction chapter is 2,000 to 5,000 words.

The rule of thumb is that anything between 40,000 words to 100,000 words is considered a novel. Below are some more specific guidelines. Keep in mind these are estimates.

Tip-The average length of a non-fiction chapter is about 4,000 words.

Word Counts

Non-fiction-50,000 to 75,000 words

Literary and Women's Fiction-80,000 to 90,000

Historical Fiction-80,000 to 100,000

Novellas-20,000 to 40,000 words

Short-Story-1,500 to 20,000 words

Mainstream Romance-50,000 to 100,000 words

Science Fiction-90,000 to 120,000 words

Thrillers/Crime/Mystery-70,000 to 90,000 words

Young Adult-40,000 to 80,000 words

Children's Picture Books-300 to 800 words

Middle Grade- 20,000 to 50,000 words

Memoir-80,00 to 100,000 words

Tip: There are numerous forms of software to help writers organize their work. One of the most popular is Scrivener:

https://www.literatureandlatte.com/

Takeaways and Notes:

_____
_____
_____
_____

Types of Publishing

Tradtional

Hybrid

Self

Vanity

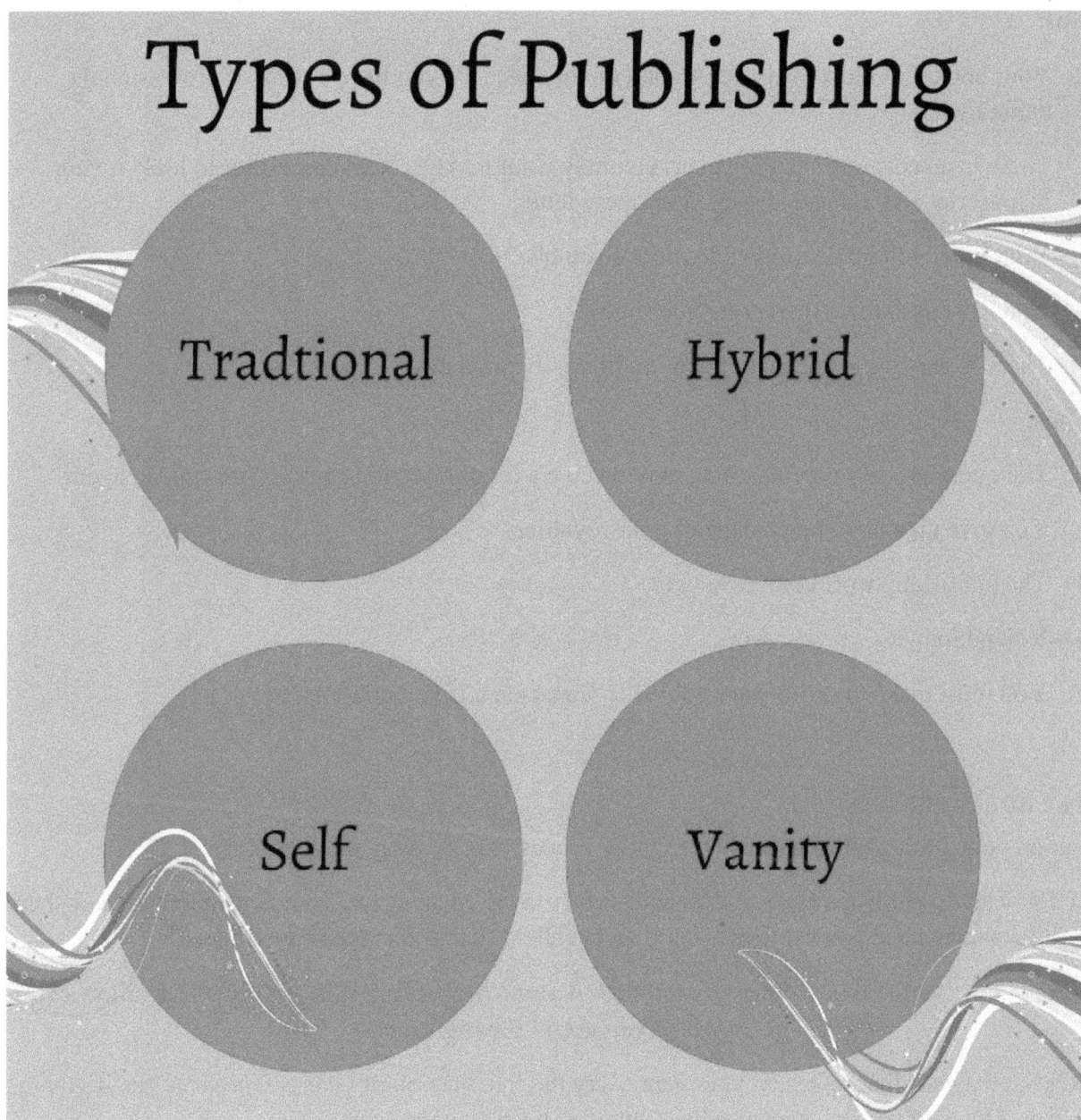

TRADITIONAL PUBLISHING:

Traditional book publishing is when a publisher offers the author a contract and, in turn, prints, publishes, and sells their book through booksellers and other retailers. The publisher essentially buys the right to publish the book and pays the author royalties from the sales. This can happen with one of the big five publishers or with a smaller independent publisher.

Tip-Don't confuse independent publishing with self-publishing. Many independent presses offer traditional publishing contracts.

Pros:

1. Your book will most likely be of good quality because you have a team of professionals behind you.

2. There is no cost upfront. However, you may want to pay a freelance editor to look at your manuscript and assist you with your query letter.

3. Your book will be distributed to more channels.

4. You have assistance marketing your book.

5. There is prestige involved in being traditionally published.

Cons:

1. The query process is brutal. You may receive a lot of rejections before you find an agent.

2. You give up a large percentage of your royalties.

3. The publishing world moves slowly.

4. You no longer own your work.

5. You must make the edits your publisher wants even if you don't agree.

THE QUERY PROCESS

Put on your adult panties because the Query Process can be long and humbling.

If you want to publish a book traditionally, you may need an agent. Some independent publishers will take unagented manuscripts. This is an excellent option for romance writers.

Tip- Don't send all of your query letters out at once. Sending it in small batches allows you to edit if you aren't having success.

Research agents that represent your genre. Try the free version of *Query Tracker* to see if you like it. The paid version is an excellent option if it fits your budget.

QueryTracker | Find literary agents and publishers with our free database

1. Every query letter needs to be individualized to the agent it is sent to you. You need to know what they are looking for, what their interests are etc. You can find this information on their website. Be sure to explain in the query letter why this agent is a good match for you.

2. Send the query out in batches of ten.

3. After you receive some feedback, rewrite your query letter.

4. Send out another batch of ten.

5. Repeat the above steps until someone says yes.

Tip- Find someone who is an expert at writing Query Letters to assist you. Many editors offer this service, and it is reasonably priced. The query letter is not an intuitive document, so it is difficult to write.

Every agent is different. You must send them exactly what they ask for. You may be asked to provide the following:

1. A query letter.

2. An elevator pitch

3. A logline

4. A short synopsis

5. A long synopsis

Tip- Some publishing houses may ask you to provide a marketing plan. The marketing section of this workbook can help you with this.

Tip: If an agent says "No," it means no. Don't ask again and whatever you do, don't beg

What is a Query Letter?

A one-page letter sent to an agent to convince them your book is worth selling.

Query Letter Example:

Nicki Pascarella

That street

That city and state

555-555-5555

Dear Ms. Smith:

When a young college professor uses her psychic abilities to solve a murder, the small town oligarchy better beware. Dr. Miranda Albright is determined to solve her mystery even as rumors and romance toss hand grenades at her. Good luck to anyone who gets in her way! I am proud to present my 87,000-word novel, *Troubles in Bellmount: A Miranda Albright, Ph.D. Mystery*. Set in 1989, in a typical small town in Western Pennsylvania, this is the first book in my steamy mystery series.

Dr. Miranda Albright's life should be perfect. She has just landed her dream job as an English professor in a small liberal arts college and has moved into a turret in her aunt's Victorian inn that overlooks the town she vacationed in as a child. Unfortunately, Miranda has a lot of problems. First and foremost, she has just stumbled over a corpse. Second, her unwanted psychic visions are strengthening, and she is the only person who knows that the wrong man was framed for the murder of the pregnant coed. More than anything, Miranda wants to fit in and feel normal, but since small-town rumors are pervasive, hiding that she is telepathic has become increasingly difficult. Finally, her love life is a mess. She may be dating a romantic knight-in-shining-armor doctor, but she can no longer ignore that the womanizing bartender she's had a crush on for years has finally noticed her. At the heart of my series is this scorching love story between Miranda and her childhood friend, Weston Westinghouse the Third.

Kaitlyn, I hope my story makes you laugh out loud and that you fall in love with the citizens of Bellmount. Readers who enjoy the storytelling style of Jana DeLeon while craving the heat of Julie Anne Long, and those who would delight in the antics of Stephanie Plum with a paranormal twist, will make the perfect audience for my novel.

I have been a high school special education teacher for three decades and a multi-award-winning Belly Dancer for the past twenty years. I have a Bachelor of Science Degree in Education of the Exceptional, with a concentration in Journalism, and my graduate work was in Psychology and American Studies. I have published articles in the Middle Eastern Dance Magazine, *Zagarette,* and on my blog, which can be found at www.thedanceofmylife.com.

The full manuscript of *Troubles in Bellmount* is available immediately. As requested, I have included the first ten pages. I look forward to hearing from you.

Sincerely,

Nicki Pascarella

What is a Logline?

A one-sentence summary or description of a book that includes the main character, setup, central conflict, and antagonist into a clear, concise teaser.

Logline Example:

Mayhem and romance abound when a college professor with psychic abilities stands up to a small-town oligarchy in order to solve a murder.

Write your Logline:

What is an Elevator Pitch?

A quick, punchy set of statements that sells your book to a publisher, agent, or reader-if the person you're trying to sell to gets into an elevator with you, you'd be able to deliver your pitch before they reach their destination.

Elevator Pitch Example:

Set in 1989 in Western Pennsylvania, the first book in my steamy mystery series tells the story of a young college professor who uses her psychic abilities to solve the murder of a pregnant coed. Miranda Albright must stand up to the corrupt town oligarchy, squelch small town rumors, and navigate her disastrous love life as she unravels the secrets around her first mystery. When considering *Troubles in Bellmount,* think Jana DeLeon with heat or Molly Harper's Half-Moon Hollow set in 1989 in Western Pennsylvania.

Write your Pitch:

What is a Short Synopsis?

About 500 words, it is a summary of your novel's plot including all the important events. It won't include subplots or minor characters.

For fun, try writing this in first and third person to see what you prefer.

Examples

Short Synopsis in First Person:

My name is Miranda Albright, and my life should be perfect. Unfortunately, I keep stumbling over corpses, and rumors and romance often toss hand grenades at me.

Let me start at the beginning. Two months ago, I began my dream job as an English professor at Bellmount College, which, according to Forbes, is the twenty-sixth most beautiful small town campus in the United States. I live ten minutes from campus in the turret of my aunt's Queen Anne Victorian Inn. My students at the college adore me, and the campus newspaper I'm the advisor for is running smoothly.

My troubles started the day I moved into town, and a perverted, porcine police officer pulled my eighteen-year-old, poop-brown monstrosity of a car to the side of the road and inappropriately touched me. Five minutes after that, I found a decaying corpse in the woods. When the wrong person was accused of the murder, I tried to persuade law enforcement that there had been a mistake. I most certainly didn't plan to go to war with the most important men in town. Since then, I have become a walking scandal. The Bellmount Bitches want to chop off my long red ringlets and feed me to an old widower. The playboy owner of the largest gun store in the state of Pennsylvania is obsessed with me, and I accidentally shot the gorgeous Weston Westinghouse III, in the behind with my 1969 bejeweled Colt Cobra Automatic.

So there you have it. Once an honor student ruled by discipline and common sense, Bellmount has turned me into an impatient risk-taker who attracts trouble like a little boy attracts dirt. I have no idea how to ditch the perverted ghost who has become my sidekick. I don't know how to convince my handsome doctor boyfriend to forgive me for recently losing my virginity to the womanizing bartender I have had a crush on for years. I can't figure out how to temper the rumors that circulate about me non-stop. One thing I know for sure is that my telepathic abilities are never wrong, and I am confident an innocent man was accused of murder. No matter how many times I get beat up, humiliated, and threatened, the town of Bellmount is going to wake up, learn the truth, and bring justice to that murdered young woman. Rest assured, I won't stop until I solve my mystery.

Short Synopsis in Third Person:

Miranda Albright's life should be perfect. Unfortunately, she keeps stumbling over corpses, and rumors and romance tend to toss hand grenades at her.

Two months ago, Miranda started her dream job as an English professor at Bellmount College. According to Forbes, Bellmount College is the twenty-sixth most beautiful small town campus in the United States. Miranda lives ten minutes from campus in the turret of her aunt's Queen Anne Victorian Inn. The happiest times of her life were the summers she spent vacationing in Bellmount with her aunt and hanging out with her cousin's best friends, West and Tommy. Tommy is a park ranger who has had a crush on Miranda since he was six. West is an incorrigible bartender who has had a hold over her since she was four. Miranda is currently dating Dr. Bradley Gordon. Brad is thirty-three and looks like the movie-star detective,

Magnum P.I. Brad is kind, brilliant, and reads her British Literature with a charming fake accent. Her students at the college adore her, and the campus newspaper she is the advisor of is running smoothly. Since she spent so much time studying, Miranda never had a best friend, and she finally has two. The first is her sassy secretary. The other is West's older cousin; although she is an air-head, she is enthusiastic and sweet.

Miranda's troubles start the day she moves into town, and a perverted porcine police officer pulls her eighteen-year-old, poop-brown monstrosity of a car to the side of the road and inappropriately touches her. Five minutes after that, she finds a decaying corpse in the woods. When the wrong person is accused of the murder, Miranda tries to persuade law enforcement there was a mistake; she didn't mean to go to war with the most important men in town. Since then, Miranda has become a walking scandal. The Bellmount Bitches want to chop off her long red ringlets and feed her to an old widower. The Playboy owner of the largest gun store in Pennsylvania is obsessed with her. Then there is the afternoon when Miranda accidentally shoots West Westinghouse III in the behind with her 1969 bejeweled Colt Cobra Automatic.

Once an honor student ruled by discipline and common sense, Bellmount has turned Miranda into an impatient risk-taker who attracts trouble like a little boy attracts dirt. She has no idea how to ditch the perverted ghost who has become her sidekick. She doesn't know how to convince her handsome doctor boyfriend to forgive her for recently losing her virginity to a womanizing bartender—or if she even wants him to. She can't figure out how to temper the rumors that circulate about her non-stop. One thing Miranda knows for sure is that her telepathic abilities are never wrong, and she is confident an innocent man was accused of murder. No matter how many times she gets beat up, humiliated, and threatened, the town of Bellmount is going to wake up, learn the truth, and bring justice to a murdered coed. Rest assured, Dr. Miranda Albright will not give up until she solves her mystery.

Notes for your Short Synopsis:

What is a Full Synopsis?

This contains more detail than the short synopsis, including character development and plot highlights. Think about summarizing each chapter in a sentence.

The Full Synopsis can be daunting. Here are a few tips:

1. Set the premise.

2. Focus on conflict.

3. Clearly outline the character's growth.

4. Focus on the plot.

5. Tell the ending.

6. Think about summing up each chapter with one sentence.

Full Synopsis Example:

It is 1989, and twenty-five-year-old DR. MIRANDA ALBRIGHT's dreams have come true. Even though her eighteen-year-old car is having mechanical difficulties and is less than aesthetic, she is thrilled as she drives to her new home in the turret of her aunt's Victorian inn. Since the age of four, Miranda has known that academia would be her life, and according to Forbes, Bellmount College is the twenty-sixth most beautiful small town campus in the United States. Miranda's fondest memories are of the summers she spent in the quaint Western Pennsylvania town with her older cousin and his best friends, TOMMY LITTLE, and the irresistible WESTON WESTINGHOUSE III.

Ten miles from town, a dishonest municipal sheriff pulls Miranda to the side of the road and wrongly accuses her of speeding. Miranda is furious when he touches her and makes a lewd proposition. After calling the officer's bluff, she composes herself and finds a piece of jewelry glinting in the sunlight. Upon picking up the creepy-looking ring, she's pulled by a magnetic force to a two-week-old decomposing corpse. The handsome DR. BRADLEY GORDON happens to drive past and comes to the distressed Miranda's aid.

Miranda uses the telepathic visions she experienced at the crime scene to conclude that the mayor, law enforcement, and most of the town council have accused the wrong man of the murder. Letting an innocent man sit in prison does not mesh with her moral code, so Miranda asks Tommy, now the local park ranger, to accompany her back to the crime scene, where she uses her powers to divine that two goons were hired to mutilate the pregnant coed's body. Miranda vows to discover who the murderer is and why his henchmen have staged the crime scene to appear like a copycat of a 1986 Satanic cult murder. A clue leads Miranda to a friendly bookie/loan shark, who lends her resources so that she can move her investigation forward.

The handsome Dr. Brad Gordon confesses that he has fallen hard for Miranda's emerald eyes, long red ringlets, and spunky personality, and they begin a sweet romance. The problem is, Miranda thinks that her perfect boyfriend may have a secret. She feels it is unethical to read his mind, but she doesn't know how to kiss him or hold his hand without hearing his thoughts. After a disastrous date, Miranda realizes she must gain control of her abilities if she is to continue with their relationship. Desperate for answers about the odd ability she inherited from her late grandmother, Miranda seeks help from a philosophical psychology professor. Her mentor guides Miranda in developing and accepting her telepathic abilities.

While navigating her love life, small-town rumors, and telepathic visions, Miranda remains obsessed with her unsolved murder mystery. Eventually, she enlists sleuthing assistance from her out-spoken colleague and an enthusiastic, air-headed waitress. As they bumble about collecting clues, the three women end up at a goldfish-eating contest at a fraternity house. They are accused of being a coven of witches in front of the First Evangelical Church's congregation. Finally, they are escorted from a swanky party at a local coal mogul's palatial mansion. Although clues gained from her sleuthing shenanigans eliminate suspects, Miranda still doesn't know who the murderer is.

As part of her investigation of the town council, Miranda decides to check out the immensely successful Grainey's Gunshop, whose owner, the playboy and town council member, GREG GRAINEY, hits on her. Despite her distaste for him and for weapons, Miranda has a strange feeling that she might need one of the latter, so she purchases a second-hand 1969 Colt Cobra. It would be a cool vintage weapon, except it has been bejeweled with pink rhinestones. When Tommy and West attempt to teach Miranda to handle her gun, she accidentally shoots West in the behind. While caring for the injured bartender, Miranda realizes the time has come for her to deal with her decade-long crush. The scorching chemistry that has been building between them leads to the loss of her virginity.

When leaving West's apartment in the middle of the night, Miranda is attacked by two thugs and divines they have been sent to scare her into dropping her murder investigation. West becomes distant as he watches Dr. Gordon care for the convalescing Miranda. Miranda heals quickly under the attentive doctor's care, but guilt over her fling with West and confusion over her feelings for him eat at her.

When her mobster friend threatens the murdered coed's father, a controlling religious leader, Miranda receives the final clue that leads her to suspect Greg Grainey. The pastor has known all along that his daughter had been sexually intimate with Grainey, but his shame and desire to protect the conservative town agenda led him to cover up the affair. When Miranda confronts Greg, she divines he accidentally strangled the coed while playing kinky games in his hot tub. Miranda also discovers that Greg capitalized on the young girl's unfortunate death, using it as an opportunity to scare people into buying weapons from his store.

She almost pays a high price for what she learns, however. Greg is holding Miranda at gunpoint when Bradley, Tommy, and West intervene. Greg, seeing no way out, commits suicide. As Brad tries to save him, Miranda discovers her boyfriend's secret. Brad has the gift of energy medicine—the ability to heal others using his empathic energy.

Miranda, joined by her menagerie—a hyperactive shetland sheepdog, a recuperating box turtle, a bratty lab rat, and Greg's perverted ghost —watch from the window seat in the high tower of her bedroom turret as the town gathers to mourn for Greg Grainey, the "beloved leader who championed their second amendment right." Miranda asks Greg why so many people helped cover up that he was the murderer. He tells her, "You have a lot to learn about small-town living, Crimson. Rumors are one thing; everyone loves a rumor. Dark secrets are another. If one secret unravels, the entire fabric of the town rips wide open, and important people go down."

Although Miranda has solved her first mystery, she is broken-hearted because the heroic Bradley Gordon has stepped away to recover from the exhaustion brought on by his special abilities. Meanwhile, the non-committal West concludes that he is in awe of Miranda's bravery and that he has fallen head over heels for her.

Notes for your Full Synopsis

A few more tips:

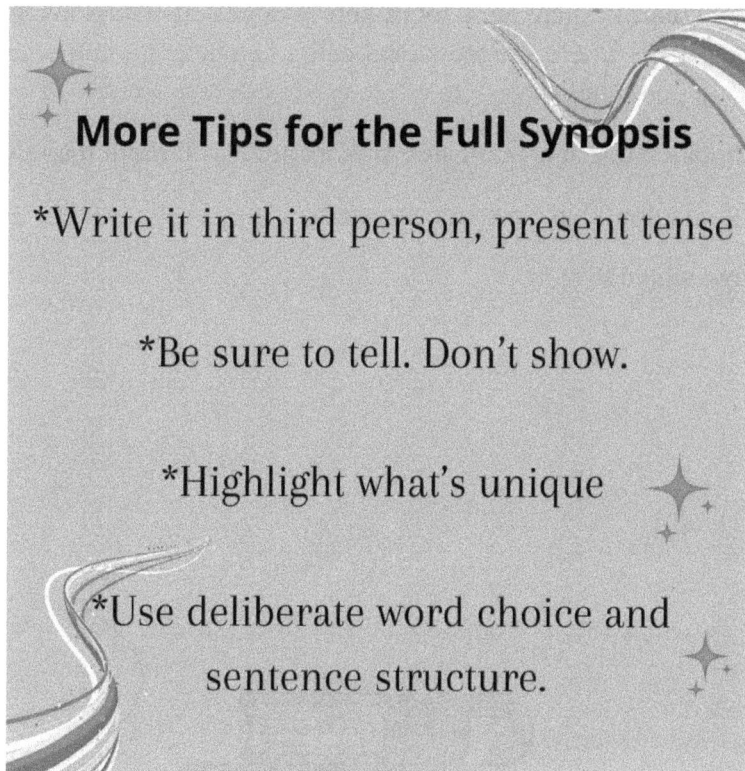

More Tips for the Full Synopsis

*Write it in third person, present tense

*Be sure to tell. Don't show.

*Highlight what's unique

*Use deliberate word choice and sentence structure.

SELF-PUBLISHING

With Self-Publishing, you handle all aspects of publishing, including editing, cover design, layout, and marketing. You can find people on Fiverr to assist with some of this. Beware, not all of these people are qualified. Many authors who have been traditionally published, and have a large audience, can switch to self-publishing and earn more in royalties. Some traditional publishers and agents will work with self-published authors, but some won't. If you self-publish and don't have good sales, it can affect an agent taking you on.

Tip-If you decide to self-publish, make sure you hire a professional editor and cover designer.

Pros:

1. You keep all of the royalties.

2. There is a sense of pride if your project is successful.

3. You have control over your content.

4. You control the time frame.

Cons:

1. There is no quality control. There are a lot of poorly done self-published books. Your book may not be ready. This is where a professional editor can help. Of course, not all self-published books are poor quality.

2. It is hard to sell books. Most self-published authors never sell more than two hundred books.

3. It can be lonely if you don't have a support system.

4. You may not know where to start.

What is an ISBN?

Every book requires a unique ISBN (International Standard Book Number). This a numeric identifier used around the world to identify books. If you plan to sell your book in a bookstore, through an online retailer, or to your local library, you'll need to have one.

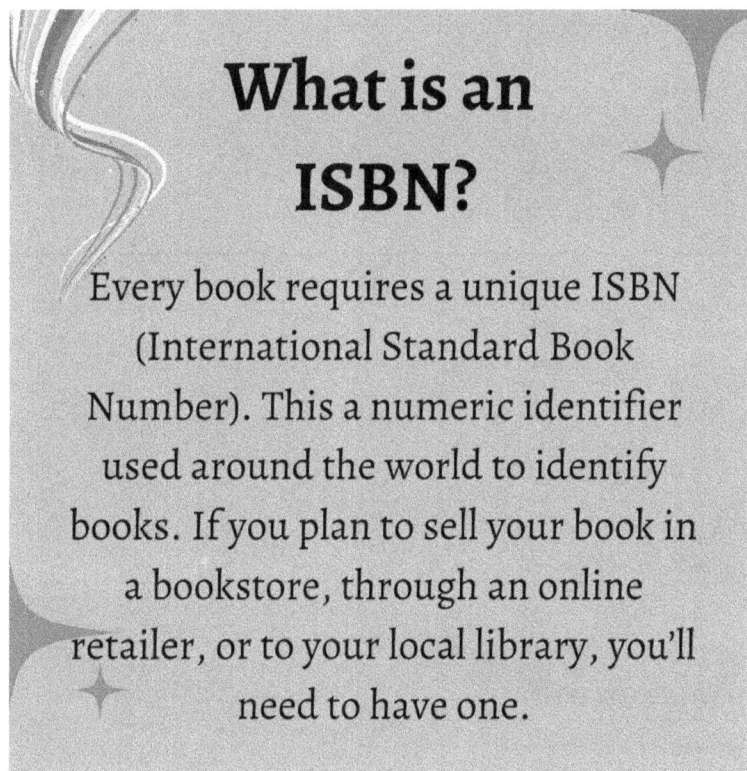

KDP will assign your book a free ISBN. If you plan to distribute your book anywhere else, you need to purchase your own ISBN. If you plan to publish more than one book, and you want to distribute it places other than Amazon, purchase your ISBN from Bowker. Bowker offers package deals.

Bowker Home Page

KDP: KINDLE DIRECT PUBLISHING WITH AMAZON

KDP is user-friendly and free. To get started, click on the website below and explore. The most challenging part is setting up your cover.

Website:

https://kdp.amazon.com/

The following is a great resource to learn about KDP:

KDP University (amazon.com)

Getting Started. KDP Quick View Activity

1. Set a timer for twenty minutes.

2. Click on the link above.

3. Look around and explore.

4. List five things that you learned below.

KDP Quick View

Today I Learned:

*

*

*

*

*

I still have the following questions:

*

*

*

*

*

Be sure to set up a profile on Author Central. It allows your followers to keep up to date on what you are doing:

https://kdp.amazon.com/

KDP Select is a free 90-day program for Kindle eBook. It allows you to reach more readers through Amazon and Kindle promotions. All authors and publishers, regardless of where they live, are eligible. Be aware if you use this, you can't have your eBook with other distributors.

Set up Kindle Countdown Deals and free book promotions with your KDP select books. Only one promotion can be used per enrollment period.

Why Use IngramSpark?

If you plan to distribute to stores other than Amazon, then IngramSpark provides you with the most connections. Most other Print On Demand services go through Ingram, so by using IngramSpark, your book can be purchased by brick-and-mortar bookstores and libraries. The cost to set up each book on Ingramspark is $49.00.

The Golden Combo

Try using KDP and IngramSpark. You set books up on KDP first because it is easier. It provides a chance to work out any kinks in books. It is much easier to make edits on KDP. One month after release, set up your title on IngramSparks. Many publishers choose to set up on IngramSparks first, then KDP picks the book up. Be aware if you use Amazon free eBook promotions, you can't publish your eBook anywhere else.

IngramSpark: Self-Publishing Book Company | Print & Distribute

The dark side of KDP

KDP is a way to get your information to readers, but it does have a dark side. If Amazon becomes a monopoly, they can raise prices on books, making a large profit while paying authors less. This could affect editors, graphic designers, and publishing houses. Amazon is making it difficult for independent bookstores to remain in existence. Additionally smaller publishers who have a history of working with and supporting authors are going under in mass. In some cases, Amazon controls the content that readers access. We all know, living in Orwell's, tyrannical world would be terrifying. And let's be clear, if any Tom, Dick or Mary can put out their unedited slop, the quality of publishing is going downhill. So, although publishing with KDP has benefits, there is also a terrifying dark side that can't be ignored. So, how can authors keep Amazon from becoming too powerful and do their part to keep the written word high quality?

First and foremost, support your local Independent Bookstores and Indie Publishing Houses!

Second, explore other options for self-publishing. See below

Third, don't publish without professional editing services.

B&N Press

Publishing with Barnes and Noble is a great option. Formerly NOOK Press, B&N Press is a free, and easy-to-use service created by Barnes & Noble.

<u>Self-Publishing for Books & eBooks | B&N Press (barnesandnoble.com)</u>

Google Books

<u>Publish and sell books with iBooks Author - Apple Support</u>

KOBO

<u>Kobo Writing Life | Rakuten Kobo</u>

Up and Coming Companies that allow you to print on demand

BookBaby	Good with customer support.	https://www.bookbaby.com/
Draft2Digital Print	Still in beta but the rumors so far are promising.	Draft2Digital
Blurb	Offers users the ability to create both standard print books and visual images.	https://www.blurb.com/

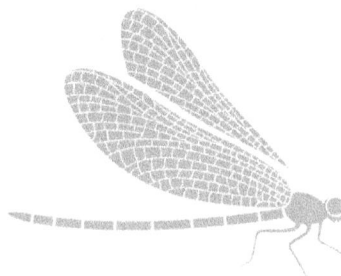

What Is A Book Blurb?

A short description of 150-200 words written for promotional purposes.

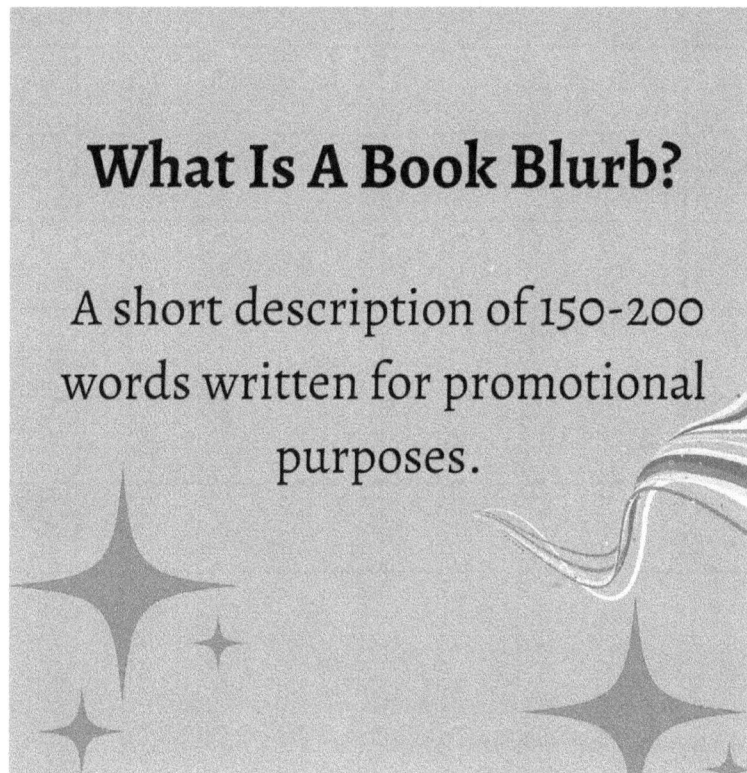

A blurb can help make or break your book and is a critical part of publishing. There are professional editors who will help you write one.

Perfecting Your Blurb:

1. Start with an attention-grabbing hook.

2. Write 1-2 short sentences that relate to the theme or plot of your book.

3. End your blurb on a cliffhanger to keep the reader interested.

4. Write the blurb in the same tone as the book.

What are your five favorite books in the genre you write? Go to the bookstore or get on Amazon and read their descriptions. Make notes below on what you think works and doesn't work.

My Favorite Books	Their Blurbs	What works	What doesn't work
1.			
2.			
3.			
4.			
5.			

KEY WORDS

1. Amazon allows you to choose seven keywords of fifty characters or less to describe your book to potential buyers. These should be relevant to your content. Don't repeat your title category or description in these keywords.

2. Combine keywords in a logical order. Customers search for *military science fiction* but probably not for *fiction science military*.

3. Before publishing, search using keywords you're considering. If you don't like the results, make changes.

4. Pretend you are the one buying the book. What search words would you look up?

5. Change keywords every eight weeks if you don't have the sales you would like.

HYBRID PUBLISHING

Hybrid publishing is an alternative to self-publishing. Authors publish their book on their own by contracting out specific services such as editing or cover design. With hybrid publishing, the author pays the publisher a fee upfront to offset the costs of production. Some Hybrid Publishers allow you to choose from a menu, so you only pay for the services you need.

Pros:

1. You keep your royalties.

2. You have more control over your publishing schedule.

3. You control your content.

4. You have a team of experts to help you.

Cons:

1. It is expensive, and you must put up a lot of money upfront. You may never recover all of these expenses.

2. You need to make sure you have a quality, respected Hybrid Publisher.

3. You may have to stay on top of the people assigned to you.

4. You have to make sure you have a Hybrid Publisher and not a Vanity Press.

Tip: Stay away from Vanity Presses.

Review the information in the self-publishing section to assist you with Hybrid Publishing. You will be paying someone to guide you through the process.

VANITY PRESSES

When working with a vanity press the author pays the publishing company upfront to edit, layout, and design their book. They often must purchase hundreds of books without marketing assistance. This type of publishing doesn't have a good reputation and is riddled with scam artists.

So, you think you are ready to publish?

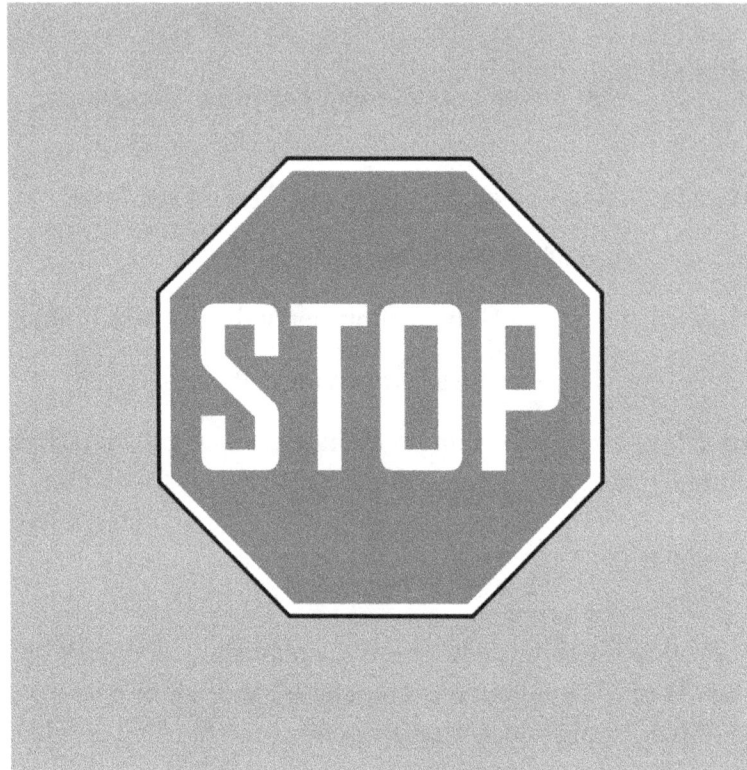

Answer these questions:

1. Have you Established a Brand? Set up Social Media Accounts? Made a Website? Started a blog? More on Establishing a Brand to follow.

2. Do you have/need a Pen Name? You may want a pen name for each of the genres you write in:

   https://www.tckpublishing.com/how-to-create-pen-name/

3. Have you let your book percolate for at least a month?

4. Have you used two to three Beta Readers?

   Tip- It is essential to let a book sit between edits. A month is ideal. Never send a just-finished manuscript out.

What are Beta Readers?

They are trusted people who read your draft and give you feedback. They can be friends, experts in the fields, or people you meet in writer groups.

5. Have you joined writers' groups and critique groups?

    Tip- Connect with other authors. Instagram is a great place to do this. Offer to do a beta read and an ARC read so that you understand the process.

6. Have you hired a professional editor? If not, stop! You should never publish a book that hasn't had a professional edit!

    Tip- Start your own Writer's Group.

What Are The Types of Editing?

Proofreading -basic spelling and grammar checks

Copyediting –happens before proofreading

Line editing-deeper edits to make sure every sentence is as effective as it can be.

Rewriting & Ghostwriting -are more writing than editing

Sensitivity Editor-looks for offensive content, stereotypes, and bias.

Author/ Editor, Therese Arkenberg, has a Fabulous Website with editing tips:

http://theresearkenberg.com/

12 Words to (Almost Always) Cut | Story Addict (theresearkenberg.com)

SELF-EDITING CHECKLISTS:

Type the following words into your search/find to see if you have overused them. You should cut as many as you can.

Title_____

Word	Check when Completed	Chapters Used	Number	Notes
very				
really				
watched				
noticed				
appeared				
totally				
completely				
absolutely				
literally				
start				
begin/began/ begun				
definitely				
certainly				
probably				
actually				
down				

up				
slowly				
quickly				

The following words are okay in moderation.

shrugged				
nod				
sighed				
reached				
wondered				
pondered				
think/thought				
felt				
realized				
understood				
that				
then				
breathed				
breath				
What words do you overuse? Add below.				

Here is a checklist you can use after each chapter.

Chapter Checklist

☐ Have I advanced the plot?

☐ Does the character accomplish the goal?

☐ Have I hooked the reader?

☐ How did the character change from the beginning to the end?

   -Internal

   -External

☐ Did I advance world-building?

☐ Did I advance other characters?

☐ Did I Show instead of Tell?

☐ Is the pace too fast? Too slow?

☐ Did I balance the scene and sequence?

-dialogue

 -actions

 -thought and emotion

☐ Did I tighten up my writing?

What would you like to add to your checklist?

☐

☐

☐

☐

☐

Make a list of issues in between each edit. This is an example of the notes Nicki made between the first and second edits of her book, *Troubles in Bellmount*. She did at least five full edits before landed a contract with her first-choice publishing house.

Tip-Create your own notes to help you edit.

Example: Nicki's Edit Notes

1. Longer chapters.

2. Better transitions.

3. Miranda more spunk early on

4. Strengthen POV

5. Show vs tell

6. Sensitivity issues-? Where are my trigger areas? Do I want them to be triggers or not?

7. Edit! Edit! Edit!

8. Strong verbs

9. Specific nouns and adjectives

10. Sensory details, every scene, smell, touch, feel, hear and see

11. Dialogue and tags.

12. Did I create a movie?

13. Did I build a band?

14. Find two new beta readers.

15. Find an editor. Ask them to complete in one month and save up so that I can afford.

You are finally ready to publish your book.

What will you do? Traditionally Publish? Self-Publish? Hybrid Publish?

What have you decided? Discuss Below:

_____
_____
_____
_____
_____
_____

Everyone you talk to will give you advice. Have you heard the following?

"You aren't a real writer if you don't traditionally publish with a big-time agent."

"You're crazy if you don't self-publish because then you get to keep your royalties.

"Hybrid publishing costs a lot of money."

Here's a great solution!

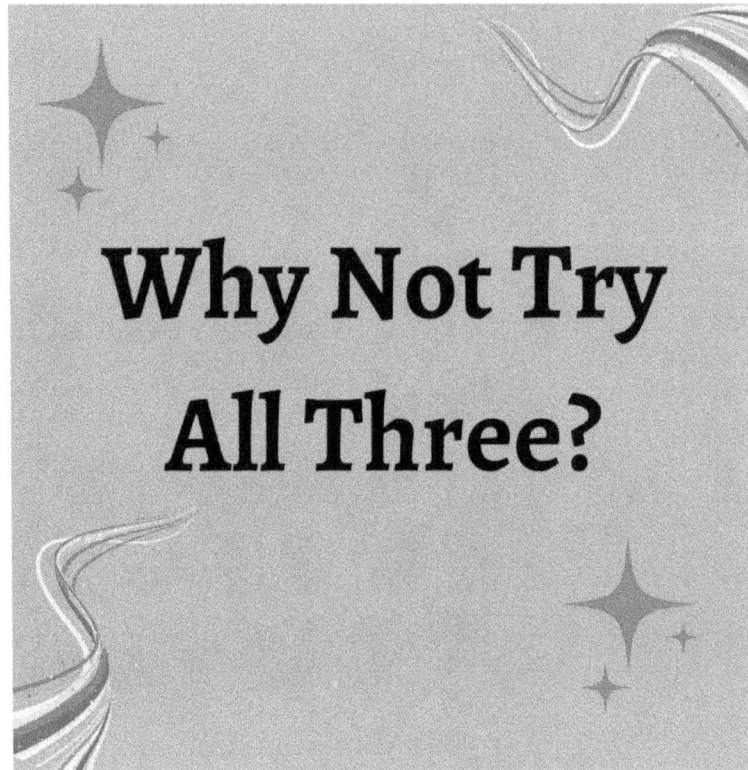

Do you have a book that lends itself to self-publishing? Go for it. Put it out there. Learn the ropes. Need some help? Hire a Hybrid Publisher to get you started. Meanwhile, write that next book and query it to agents.

MY PUBLISHING PLAN:

What are your first five steps?

1._____

2._____

3._____

4._____

5._____

Notes:

_____
_____
_____
_____
_____
_____
_____
_____
_____
_____
_____

NOTES:

B efore you start, establish your brand!

BRANDING

As an author, you are the brand of your book. Even if you publish with a traditional publishing house, they will require you to market your brand and your book. A potential reader will not buy your book because it is #2689 on Amazon. Readers need a connection to purchase a book.

Tip-A Brand Can Be Anything!

Your brand should evoke emotion. It should be consistent with your titles and be consistent with your online presence.

We are used to thinking about brands in relation to companies and products (The golden arches of McDonald's or the simple logo of Apple). Nowadays, anything can be a brand. Even as an individual, you have a personal brand. So, what is your personal brand? Whether you're known for your snaps, or you're still using a typewriter, you have a brand that exists both on and offline. Luckily, there are great tools and resources to help you with the personal branding process. Use them to leave the right impression on people who look you up online.

The idea of personal/professional branding makes some people uncomfortable. But, if you don't take control of your personal brand online, you are missing out on opportunities and letting others control your narrative. While the specific circumstances and goals vary by entrepreneur, the overall concepts and process are still applicable to every entrepreneur.

PERSONAL BRANDING

Without a story behind your brand, your book is just an inanimate object. A story elicits a connection with your audience and has the power to bring you and your vision alive.

It just so happens that personal branding is an obsession of Julie's. She gets the obligatory eye roll when she presents the question, "What is your personal brand"? She is met with responses such as, "I don't need personal branding" or "This is an uncomfortable space. It seems so narcissistic." The truth of the matter is, if you don't control your brand, others will. People make judgments based on how you present yourself. Therefore, you create a personal brand just by existing.

Personal branding is an essential cog of the professional branding machine and is the essence of who you are as an entrepreneur. By embracing your brand, you live this brand intrinsically and extrinsically. Your core values and beliefs are directly reflected in how you present and manage your professional identity. So, personal branding and professional branding are one and the same. To further clarify, branding is an illustrative description of what you, as a human, represent. Do you represent integrity? Are you creative? Maybe you have a bohemian heart? The list is endless.

Exercise: Take a minute to pause and write down three cornerstone phrases that represent you.

1._____
_____

2._____
_____

3._____
_____

Analyze these key phrases and articulate how they distinguish you in a personal and in your professional ecosystem.

Conduct effective market research. Market research is important because there is no such thing as an original idea. Check out people in your genre who you admire.

Who are these writers?

1._____

2._____

3._____

4._____

5._____

Study these writers and answer the following questions.

1. What do you like and dislike about their brand?

_____

_____

2. Before making significant branding efforts, you will first have to answer a few key questions. Are customers aware of your brand? How can you authentically express your brand to connect with your target audience?

_____

_____

_____

3. Focus on a unique value proposition. Your brand is your promise to the customer. What is your promise?

_____

_____

4. Choose a brand that delivers your message clearly. Once you have identified your reader's interests and desires and have come up with a strategy to engage them, it's time to clearly articulate your service to help solve their problem. List ideas for your brand name below.

_____

_____

_____

Tip-If your book is nonfiction, your writings will solve a potential problem for your readers. If your book is fiction, your writings will elicit escape and create a fantasy they will be engaged in.

5. Create an emotional connection. Psychologists have found that 90% of communication is non-verbal. How will you relay your message visually? Sketch on the next page.

6. Deliver consistent communications. Once an author has developed an effective brand and identity strategy, it must be implemented consistently through every "point of contact" with readers. Brainstorm various points of contact that your potential reader will engage with your branding.

_____

_____

_____

_____

_____

_____

_____

_____

_____

_____

_____

Your audience craves an experience. Whether you are writing fiction or nonfiction, with every word you engage a reader with your expertise. To engage your readers, you need to know your readers. Deconstructing your readers from the inside out is an important exercise.

Reader Avatar Exercise: Play around with the idea of defining your reader. Become intimate with their likes, dislikes, fears, and desires. Try to understand their motivations. This may be a challenging task, but it can also be a lot of fun.

Demographics to Consider When Determining your Reader Avatar

Gender

Age

Race

Religion

Household income

Education level

Do they have children, how many

Marital status

Location

Describe your Readers:

Visibility Of Your "Brand" (Book)

★ A Branded Website ★ Facebook Business ★ Facebook Lives ★ Email List ★ Your Reputation ★ Instagram ★ Instagram Live ★ Clubhouse ★ Pinterest 54 ★ Press Releases ★ Podcasts (court podcasts to be a guest) ★ Community Involvement ★ Networking ★ A website (WordPress, Wix, or Shopify) ★ Google Business ★ Google Ads ★ YouTube Channel ★ Partnerships With Other Companies ★ Media (features on your service/ product) ★ SEO Management (Search Engine Optimization) ★ Etsy Shop ★ Ebay ★ Online Course Creation ★ Blogging ★ TikTok ★ Linktree

GETTING YOUR MESSAGE TO THE MASSES:

Website- Don't even think about launching your book without a website. Building a website that reflects your brand is the cornerstone of your books' visibility. Without a solid website, you will lose credibility and potential readers. Because Google can make or break any creative venture, elevating your brand on a personal website helps boost the likelihood of readers finding your book.

This doesn't mean you have to spend thousands of dollars on a larger-than-life platform. It means that your brand needs to hold space on the internet as a reference for your customers. This is something you can do on your own or hire a professional. Julie is a self-taught web designer who explored various hosting sites until she got it right. Her go-to website builder is Wix. It is user-friendly and has a large variety of templates that you can choose from. If you are selling products, Shopify is a wonderful tool to display and sell your products. Other popular platforms are Square Site, WordPress, and GoDaddy. And if the mere mention of building your own website, has you quaking in your boots, hire out a designer. Don't be afraid to ask for help. Julie frequently dips into the freelancer pond when she is stuck or has limited time. Freelance designers flood sites like Fiverr and Upwork. Simply list your requirements and budget, and you will have experts knocking on your door. Find a designer who understands your vision, has excellent references, and has the time to walk you through the design process. Just be careful you don't get scammed.

Launch A Podcast- Launching a podcast can be a daunting idea. However, it is a powerful platform to facilitate the voice of your book. If you don't have the bandwidth to launch a podcast of your own, pitch your book to podcasts that your potential readers listen to. It also adds a layer of credibility to your coaching business since it positions you as a thought leader and expert in your field.

PODCATING FOR AUTHORS

As an author you need to have your voice heard. What better way to send your message out to the universe than with a podcast? You have the option to start one of your very own or pitch other podcasts to be a guest. There is a magical quality when you slip your earbuds in and are greeted by the familiar riffs of a podcast host. You are transported into another world that sparks imagination, creativity, and ideas.

Podcasting is making a resurgence in popularity. According to the Intelligencer, the reason podcasts may be growing is that the economics are compelling. Producing an average podcast costs far less than producing a TV show or a radio show. All you really need is a microphone or two, a copy of Audacity or some other editing software, and a cheap hosting service for the audio files themselves.

Not only will you bring a new audience to your books, podcasting can produce income! Advertising rates on a successful podcast are big enough to pay for the costs many times over. Several top podcasters have stated that their CPM (cost to an advertiser per thousand impressions, a standard ad-industry unit) was between $20 and $45. Compare that to a typical radio CPM (roughly $1 to $18) or network TV ($5 to $20) or even a regular old web ad ($1 to $20), and the podcast wins.

STARING YOUR OWN PODCAST

Step 1: Choose a topic you love. Just like blogging, you need to select a niche for your podcast that provides information that is in high demand with listeners.

Step 2: Pick a podcast title. A podcast title can help the listener anticipate the content and purpose of your podcast.

Step 3: Write a sound description. Again, you are a writer, so writing an illustrative description of your podcast should be a piece of cake. Remember, you should write a descriptive paragraph about the contents of your show to entice listeners.

Step 4: Hire someone to create your artwork. The podcast will require some artwork or a square image that represents your show and the niche it belongs to. Canva can help with this. Download the app Anchor.FM (for free) and start playing around. There are dozens of podcast hosting platforms, so do your research. Anchor.FM is a great tool to practice on and get familiar with how to podcast. If you have a little money to invest in podcasting, Podetize is a preferred platform. It allows you to have up to 5 podcasts per account with unlimited bandwidth. Plus, it boasts terrific customer support and a reasonable price point.

Tip: Anchor FM is a good place to start. www.anchor.fm Anchor is a free app that is super easy to navigate. You can record, edit, and publish your podcast with ease.

Branding

Branding can be a fun adventure that evokes creativity and clarity. Do the research, understand market trends, and take the leap into thinking outside the box. Do branding a little bit differently and you will reap exponential rewards!

OTHER CREATIVE WAYS TO BOOST VISIBILITY:

Affiliations-Partner with other authors and team up to promote similar visions. This will exponentially increase the audience of both ventures.

Collaboration-The power of two doubles visibility. Find ambitious authors who would love to collaborate on a project. You will gain visibility through their audience and vice versa. These connections will be an invaluable resource as you further your coaching career

Online Course Creation and Workshops-An online course or workshop is proof that you are an expert on a topic. There is no better way to gain notoriety as a thought leader and writer than creating an online course or holding an interactive workshop. Perhaps you are an expert in nutrition, creativity, or self-help, the platform of online courses creates visibility and a passive stream of income.

Swag-Everybody loves free stuff. Nothing gets the attention of a prospective client faster than a free t-shirt, hat, or notebook that is embroidered with your logo. Consider swag in your repertoire of visibility hacks. This is a critical yet straightforward cog in connecting with clients. It can be as simple as a business card or as elaborate as customized samples to give to your clients, pre-sale. It endears customers to your brand and is a reminder that they can't live without your service or product. Customized merch creates a brand presence and doesn't have to cost a fortune. My go-to favorite is www.discountmugs.com. I have used this site to customize mugs, pens, shirts, and journals. My clients are always giddy with excitement when they receive a personalized gift with a note that expresses my gratitude for their trust in me. www.printful.com Julie is obsessed with Printful. It is an easy way to make a statement that your clients will remember. Printful is an on-demand printing and warehousing company that helps people turn their ideas into brands and products. Whether you wish to create your own online brand or give someone a personalized t-shirt, it's super easy to customize tee shirts, stickers, mugs, and more. Printful is full service. They automatically receive the order, fulfill, and ship. You can literally do it in your sleep.

A Free Sneak Peak-Creating visibility simply means sharing your vision. Free content is an extension of your vision and will create trust and a reputation with your future customers on an intimate level. What does Free Content Mean? Many experts exclaim, "Know your worth-don't give yourself and your services away for free." While the concept of understanding your self-worth is important, giving away free things can help build your brand. When you are starting off you may need to work for free. This could establish you as a writer, and ultimately lead to referrals and reviews. Think about posting a chapter on your blog. Give away free books to reviewers.

Grow Your Reach-Nourish the community you serve by getting involved. Offer to do beta reviews and ARC reviews for other authors. Share their book releases on social media. Attend their book signings.

Charitable Partnerships-Julie champions every capable human to give their time, services, resources, and expertise to those in need. This philanthropic act should be executed with no intention other than to make the world a better place. The noble act of volunteering does have added benefits. You make connections, network, and allow people to witness your overall mission.

Contest or Challenge Pre-launch-This is a savvy move to offer an attention-getting challenge. At the end of the challenge, offer a package or product to the grand-prize winner. Contests drum up unexpected excitement about your new business. It takes time to prepare and execute your pre-launch. However, when you emit extra energy, the enthusiasm is contagious

YouTube Channel-Even if you aren't camera-ready, turn on your smartphone and give YouTube a try. Not only is YouTube a platform that garners increased visibility, but the website will also boost your rating on Google. Google is the gold standard of search engines.

Paid Advertising-Google Ads-Google is an entity unlike any other. Whether you like it or not, it is a necessary evil. Dabble in Google Ads. You can pay as little as $3.00 a day to start creating a rhythm of website visitors. Don't dismiss the behemoth that is Google. Make friends with this search engine, because Google has the power to elevate your business or eliminate it.

Pinterest- Don't be fooled by this unassuming powerhouse of a search engine. Many users are misinformed about Pinterest's power, and they often label it "social media." This platform is Google in disguise. Pinterest attracts users that are in the discovery phase of a search. Users are looking for recipes, or clothing, and even inspiration in their lives. And the amazing part of the user experience is that users are poised to purchase. The algorithms are such that content can be used and reused, unlike social media platforms. The Pinterest algorithm soaks up current pins. For example, if it is February, pins that smack of Valentine's Day love and tend to garner more interest.

How do you start on Pinterest? Use your Canva account to create appealing visuals that aren't blatant advertisements. First, think about your desired audience and ask yourself, what would this audience be interested in? Draw in your audience with a visually appealing display of something you represent. For example, a client who happens to own a bakery should post a recipe or a photo of a decadent pastry. This expands visibility. Remember, visibility is the key to establishing your brand.

Why Pinterest Works

When you draw a client in with your vibrant pin, you have the opportunity to expand on this pin in your content. When a user clicks on the pin, it immediately takes them to your website. This provides a one-step process. A photo and simple content attract a user; then, they are swept to your website, where you can elaborate on your life-altering product or service. The simple 1-click step of getting a user to your website will lead to client engagement and a possible sale. (Remember, simple is better. The more a user is required to navigate different platforms, the more likely you will lose their attention.)

What's Even Better? If a Pinterest user pins one of your pins to their board, all of their followers will experience your brand. Pinterest has the capability to expand your visibility exponentially. Hustler's Tip: Budget a little money to invest in Pinterest Ads. You can budget as little as two dollars a day, and your pins will be seen. Julie's website hits doubled in the first week of testing out this marketing strategy. The demographics of Pinterest are 80% women who possess untapped buying potential. She typically curate her pins to be female-centric. Curate your Pins specifically to your reading audience.

Press Release-Sharpen your Number 2 pencil and start writing. Write a short snippet on why your business will change the world. Remember, it must be newsworthy, so craft a vignette of why it is crucial that the community learns of your work. Once all the T's are crossed and the I's are dotted, search local papers, magazines, and media outlets that may be interested in your story. Look for a page on their website that allows for press release submissions. Send your story their way and sit back and wait for your inbox to start clamoring for more! Press Releases are another amazing vehicle to gain visibility and boost your ranking in Google.

Tip: Use EIN Presswire to distribute releases. With one click of the mouse, your press release will be sent to dozens of media outlets. www.einpresswire.com

PITCHING A PODCAST

Podcast Pitches- Ask yourself, what podcasts your potential customers listen to. Once you have narrowed down a list of podcasts, email them the undeniable reasons they should feature you. Make this pitch short and poignant. Distinguish yourself as a leader in the industry and be very clear about why you will empower their audience. Add links to your website, press, and anything powerful that states that you are a credible thought leader in this niche. Remember to make your contact information easily accessible so they can reach out with one click. Also, keep it brief.

Checkout Pitch Podcasts: www.pitchpodcasts.com

STARTING A PODCAST:

Step 1: Choose a topic you love. Just like blogging, you need to select a niche for your podcast that provides information that is in demand with listeners.

Step 2: Pick a podcast title. A podcast title can help the listener anticipate the content and purpose of your podcast.

Step 3: Write a sound description. Again, you are a writer, so writing an illustrative description of your podcast should be a piece of cake. Remember, you should write a descriptive paragraph about the contents of your show to entice listeners.

Step 4: Get your artwork created. The podcast will require some artwork or a square image that represents your show and the niche it belongs to. Canva is a great tool to use for this.

More tips:

Download the app Anchor.FM (for free) and start playing around. There are dozens of podcast hosting platforms, so do your research. Anchor.FM is a great tool to practice on and get familiar with how to podcast.

If you have a little money to invest in podcasting, Podetize is a preferred platform. It allows you to have up to 5 podcasts per account with unlimited bandwidth. Plus, it boasts terrific customer support and a reasonable price point.

Simplifying SEO Management/ Search Engine Optimizations-Are inextricably linked to brand visibility. The topic of SEOs is complex, yet so simple. Figure out what your potential client will type in a search engine to find you. Once you have tapped into your future reader's mind, use these keywords in all the content you produce. For example, smatter these keywords all over your website. Sprinkle them in your social media, in your press releases, and everything you send out into cyberspace.

SEO is the process of optimizing your website, pages, blog posts, and more for search engines like Google. If you understand it and do it right, you can get a significant amount of traffic from search engines. In other words, when people use Google to search for specific terms, your site will show up near the top of the results. People will click on your site and read your awesome content. Pretty simple, right? Well, sort of. The general concept behind SEO is simple but it's a little more complicated in practice. There are trillions of web pages out there and Google must understand them and give the relevant ones to searchers. One of the primary goals of SEO is to make your website stand out from everything else. You want to make your site as appealing as possible to Google. The more appealing it is, the more it will be shown to searchers and the more traffic you'll get. So, how do you make your site stand out in the eyes of Google?

Try Keywords Everywhere to understand SEOs. This is a chrome extension and has a very low price point. There are a lot of options to explore on the internet, so remember to keep it simple. It is priced at a relatively low at a $10 price point and has been a game-changer in SEO repertoire.

Branding

Branding can be a fun adventure that evokes creativity and clarity. Do the research, understand market trends, and take the leap into thinking outside the box. Do branding a little bit differently and you will reap exponential rewards!

Moz Rank Checker | Check Mozrank Score of A website (smallseotools.com)-Is one more tool to analyze your website viability. This tool can help you with your SEO ranking. Moz Rank is one of the most popular and dependable metrics if you want to measure the authority of a domain or web page. Moz created the metric "Mozrank" to calculate the search engine optimization rating of a certain web page or a website. Many webmasters and SEO experts are using Moz Rank as a point of reference for optimizing search engines. Mozrank score is calculated between 1 to 10 on a scale. 10 is the highest score on the scale and 1 is the lowest Moz rating. The Moz ranking of a certain web page is based on the popularity of the pages that are linked to them. This would also mean that if the MozRank of the linking pages is high, there is a greater chance that the MozRank of the receiving page of those links will be high too.

SEO BRAINSTORM-What search words will your potential client google to find you? It is imperative that you curate keywords that are highly searched but have limited competition.

What are some keywords you will use for SEO management?

Public Speaking-This can be a scary topic. Some lucky individuals grab a microphone with ease, but for many of us it is the biggest fear in our lives. We, as authors, are the creators of our literary works, so we are deemed the expert. The art of speaking to the masses is one we need to perfect to garner a bigger audience. Public speaking for authors can look like book signings, zoom webinars, speaking at live events or doing a Facebook/ Instagram live. The more you speak the more you gain the trust of your audience.

Engaging new readers takes time. It is important to establish a relationship with potential readers prior to monetizing.

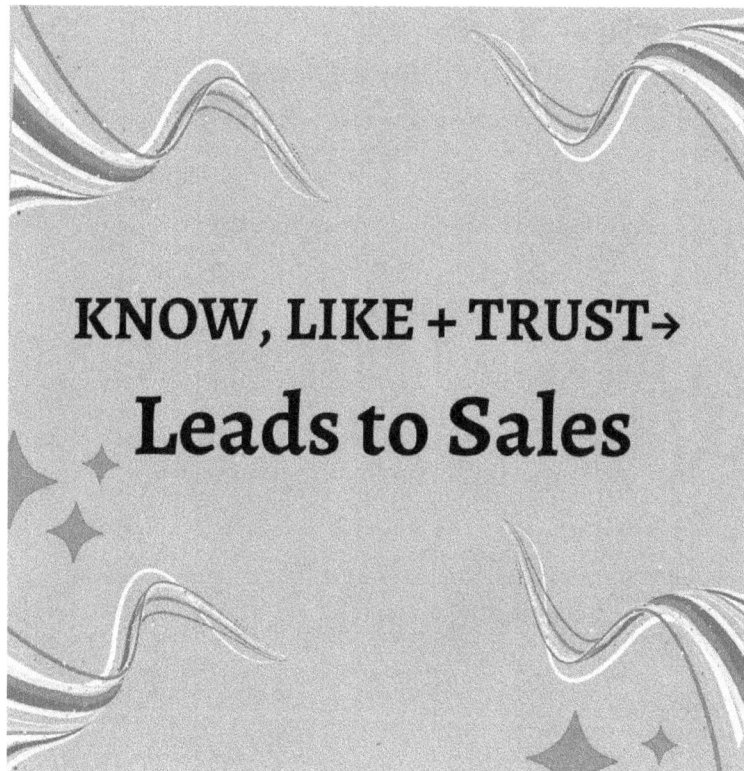

KNOW, LIKE + TRUST→
Leads to Sales

CLUBHOUSE FOR AUTHORS
What the heck is Clubhouse?

Clubhouse is an audio-only social media app known for its unconstrained conversations, celebrity backers, and invite-only status. The experience falls somewhere between call-in radio and professional conferences. Users select rooms based on interest, then engage in live conversation. Room moderators decide who speaks, and it's common to see rooms with dozens of active participants.

Clubhouse is LinkedIn on steroids. While LinkedIn has its place in navigating job searches, LinkedIn user engagement seems dormant. Specifically, LinkedIn is used on an as-needed basis. (I need a job, so I need to check out LinkedIn). Clubhouse, on the other hand, is a space that expands user experience by providing instant gratification. Clubhouse has provided the ground floor for job hires, shark-tank life investments, and intimate conversations to take place. This app is known for its lightning bolt conversations that facilitate networking on a scale nowhere else seen.

Clubhouse Engagement Can Lead to:

- Collaborations with influential humans that inspire others to be bold and live outside the box.
- Author/ Reader concentrated rooms that facilitate an engrossing exchange of ideas for authors
- An increase in reader engagement.
- An increase in knowledge, personal development, health and wellness, personal branding, self-actualization and much more.
- Fine-tune public speaking skills.
- Introduced and provided unprecedented access to influential public figures who have agreed to be guests on Julie's podcast, "Obsessed, With Humans On The Verge Of Change."
- Daily inspiration to do better and be better.

The best part of Clubhouse is that, when you join, you have access to limitless brain power. You can listen to live conversations on almost any topic. You can join the conversation and ask questions or pick the brains of prolific thought leaders. If this isn't enough, you can moderate your own rooms, choose the topic of conversation, and invite others to join in on impactful subject matter.

WHO SHOULD JOIN CLUBHOUSE?

All writers should do this. Now! You should dip your toe in the Clubhouse Pond and start sharing your story.

Where do you start?

Download the Clubhouse App to sign up. It may take a while to be admitted because the app creators want to keep a controlled flow of users. Or find a friend on Clubhouse and ask them to invite you. Clubhouse users are allotted a managed number of invites, that they can send to their friends. Next, play around with the app. Visit different rooms, listen in on the conversations. Join the conversation or better yet, be the conversation. Enjoy the interactive experience and be inspired daily by a cross-section of perspectives.

CURRENT TRENDS IN MARKETING

Branding and Marketing is an art that dabbles in fortune-telling. It would be great to have a crystal ball providing the exact tools to curate a marketing and branding plan that is accurate. However, marketing is not an exact science. As a brand, it is imperative that you are agile. To harness a successful brand, you need to be prepared for curveballs.

The curveballs thrown to businesses globally have been epic frustrations during the recent COVID pandemic. Consumers were relegated into digital spaces and brand building screeched to a halt. The successful brands understood the needs of their consumers and were able to rise to the top with buoyant precision.

The following list should help you keep up with these current trends:

Video-Video creates a real connection with your audience. Building your brand is akin to building relationships. It is imperative that you invest in your relationships and give your audience some facetime. This can look like live feeds on Instagram, Facebook, or Linkedin. This can be an embedded video in your email. Or it can look like lively videos on YouTube (which is owned by Google).

Video creation can seem like a big production. So, start small. Try Viddyoze. Viddyoze provides templates in which you insert art and text and it creates innovative video clips for your branding efforts.

Content is Queen-Content! Content! Content! Content can look like blogs, websites, speaking engagements, podcasts, and videos. The list goes on and on. Google-friendly content can skyrocket you to the top of search engines.

Content is the versatile engine to run the online marketing of your business. Here's what you need to know when publishing content online:

Lead with value-Giving value (free information, advice, tips) builds the credibility of your business and keeps your company at the front of consumers' minds.

Map the customer journey-Content marketing is storytelling that brings customers through the stages listed below:

Awareness-This is the stage when potential customers learn about you and your business. Lead customers from this "Awareness" stage to the next stage with a call-to-action to subscribe to your newsletter. At this stage, the content can be:
* Tutorial (from searches like Google or Pinterest)
* Viral post (something people will share or retweet)
* Expert content or analysis report

Consideration-At this stage, potential customers already know about you and would consider buying from you. They are already in your circle. Content can be half educational and half promotional. You'll reach customers at this stage via content such as newsletters, case studies, and podcasts.

Decision-At the decision stage, customers trust your business and are considering making a purchase from you. Content here isn't to educate or build brand awareness. It's to address the benefits of your products or services. At this stage, the call-to-action leads the customer to either make a purchase or start a free trial.

Experiential Branding: (GAMIFICATION)-Consumers are bored with the bombardment of advertising. The overwhelming flow of sales pitches to their inbox is a futile attempt of doing it like all the rest. Creating an experience for your audience is essential in capturing their attention and their imagination.

Gamification is the application of typical elements of game playing (point scoring, competition with others, rules of play) to other areas of activity, typically as an online marketing technique to encourage engagement with a product or service. Try this with the launch of your book. Make it a friendly competition. This is an excellent way to increase engagement and engender trust.

VISABILITY REVISITED

To start your brand-spanking-new business, you must create a vision for your brand, and how you will represent this brand to the world is critical. Elevating this vision to capture the imagination of a targeted audience can be a labor of love. The visibility pillar will establish you in the game. Visibility is a consistent cadence of creatively thinking outside the box. Start small and don't give up. The process of establishing a visible brand will distinguish you from your competitors. This process allows for trial and error, so dabble in different exercises and position your ideas on various platforms. Remember, it takes time to start seeing results, so a consistent cadence in the dissemination of your brand is a powerful way to market your book.

Pre-Book Launch

Tip-Have fun and use your imagination.

1.Set up your ARC Team of ten to fifteen people.

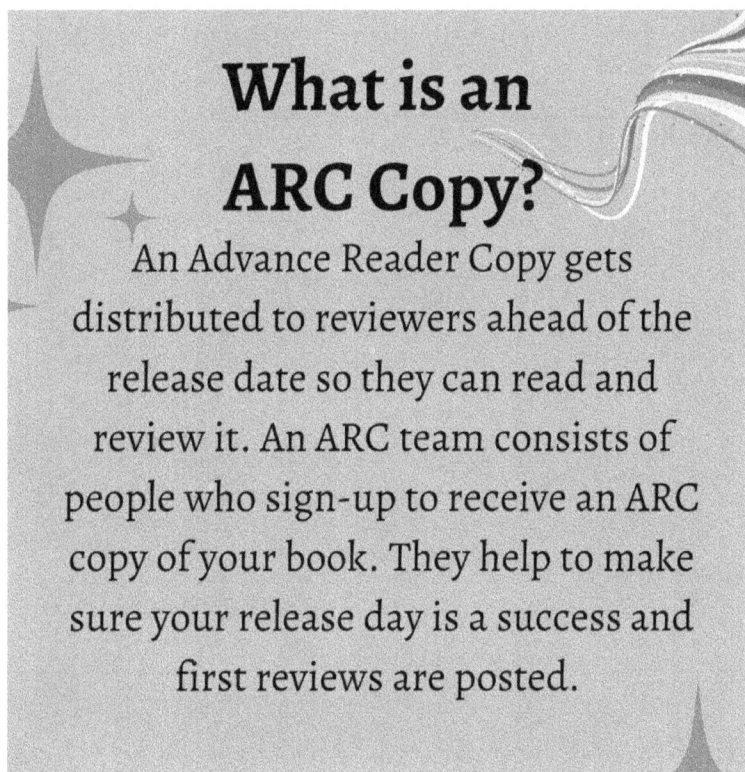

What is an ARC Copy?

An Advance Reader Copy gets distributed to reviewers ahead of the release date so they can read and review it. An ARC team consists of people who sign-up to receive an ARC copy of your book. They help to make sure your release day is a success and first reviews are posted.

Ask your team to read and post a review of the book for its launch. Some publishers will provide ARC copies for you. You can also send a PDF of your manuscript. Ask your team to post about your book on their social media feeds. Then invite them to your launch party. Finally, show them a lot of love and appreciation.

2. Do a ten-day video countdown on TikTok or IG Reels. Everyday post something about your book.

3. Have a Launch Party. These can be virtual or in person. Coffee houses are wonderful places to launch your book. Any business where the owner supports you can work. One popular author uses a vineyard.

4. Inviting friends to a Facebook live event is a great way to launch your book. You can plan an all-day party on Facebook where you do a post every thirty minutes to hour. Play games and have a guest post. Your imagination is your only limit.

5. Do an Instagram live interview.

6. Star in a podcast on your release day.

7. Host Giveaways You can do these pre-launch, on Launch day, or anytime you want. Match it with special events.

8. Swag packages are great. Include book, bookmarks, reading swag, a book memento. Your imagination is your only limit. Be careful of expenses. You don't have to spend a lot of money to have cool swag. Handmade keychains and bookmarks are perfect.

9. Have contests and play games for your giveaways. Ask people to tag your friends on social media.

Notes to plan your launch:

Tip -Caution: It is costly to mail swag packages. If you have a limited budget, make sure you do these in the country you live in.

This checklist can help whether you are traditionally or independently published.

Marketing Checklist

☐ Set up your ARC Team to review your book and assist with Social Media posts. DO NOT pay for reviews.

☐ Reveal your cover on Social Media, blog, website, etc.

☐ Plan a launch party—Facebook, Instagram Live, or an in-person event. Local coffee shops are great places to do this. You can schedule a book signing to go along with it.

☐ Do a swag package give-away on your launch day. (Unfortunately, you may have to limit this to the country you live in.)

☐ Ask your ARC team to publish reviews on your release day.

☐ Send your release information to your email list.

☐ Run promotions on The Fussy Librarian, Robins Reads, etc. (Research these carefully. Not all promotion sites are legit or worth the money.)

Free Personalized Book Suggestions | The Fussy Librarian

https://robinreads.com

☐ Pair free e-book days with other publicity. Example: Do a podcast on the day of your giveaway.

☐ Know your audience. Your book is not for everyone. Think, how can I get my marketing efforts to this audience? Example: If you have a vegan cookbook, contact local vegan groups and health food stores. Nicki's recent release had a sheltie in it, so she contacted a Sheltie influencer to do her promotional video.

☐ Your efforts must be ongoing. Schedule some type of advertising every month.

☐ Change your search categories every eight weeks.

☐ TikTok is free advertising and reaches a lot of people. Be aware that you must first have a stage persona to be successful on this app.

☐ Set your budget and stick to it. Yes, you will need a budget even if you are traditionally published.

☐ Offer to run a book club or teach a writing workshop.

☐ Support other writers! They will support you back.

Share the following information with your friends, family, and fans:

Support an Author

- Buy the book and purchase extra copies as gifts.
- Recommend the book to others.
- Review the book on major retail sites.
- Review the book on Goodreads.
- Request the local library to buy the book.
- Post about the book on social media--add lots of pictures.
- Follow the author and publisher on social media.
- Read and talk about the book in public.
- Connect with the author about speaking opportunities.
- Face the book outward in book displays.
- Blog about the book.
- Nominate the book for a book club.
- Check the book out of the library.
- Request the book in school libraries.

Tip- Keep track of the books you sell at in person events. You may need to pay taxes on these. Having a sales slip that lists the date, place, and title of the book will help you to keep track of these records.

Every author needs a professional Media Kit. The following are things to include in yours:

Author Bio-This is a series of four bios, written in different lengths to make the media's job easy. If you provide only one long bio, journalists and others who need just a short paragraph about you must wade through your bio, find what they need, and write it. This slows them down. And there's no guarantee that what they write will be accurate.

Book Synopsis-Write these all in the third person, in four different lengths: a two-line summary, short, medium, and long. Take your time to consider the full scope of the book before writing each synopsis. Consider what the book has to offer, the most compelling parts of the story, or the niche the book serves. Write short and pointed sentences that are appropriate for a general audience and pitch your book in as few words as needed.

Press Release-Include contact information, a headline and subhead. Start with the most interesting aspect of the book and explain what the reader will learn. Include a quote from the author. It can include why you wrote the book, what you hope readers will learn or advice included in the book. Include a call to action with a link to a website where readers can buy the book.

Sample Chapter-Choose a chapter that reflects what the book is about. You can include a link to a Table of Contents and Amazon reviews.

Interview Questions-Most journalists, broadcasters and bloggers who want to interview you will not have time to read your book. That's why they will welcome a list of interview questions. They won't necessarily limit the interview to those questions, but the list will provide a handy springboard that will help them start the conversation

Contact Information-Include a sheet that tells people every way possible to contact you: by office phone, email, Skype, and links to all your social media profiles. This may well be the most important item in your media kit. If you're mailing copies of your book to reviewers, it's a good idea to slip a copy of your press release and the contact information sheet into the book.

Book Review Excerpts-You should ask for book reviews before you launch the book. When you get them, choose excerpts from the best and compile them onto a sheet along with basic information about the book. These excerpts might sway a journalist to write about you. Or they might prompt someone to buy your book and maybe even write a review.

Photos-Include links to high-resolution head shots and a few environmental shots that show you in a variety of settings. For example, a cookbook might include photos of the chef in the kitchen, whipping up a favorite dish, or shopping at a local farmer's market. Small newspapers, newsletters and bloggers will welcome these photos. You will also need a photo of your book cover.

A press kit is an essential part of marketing for a every writer. It should include:

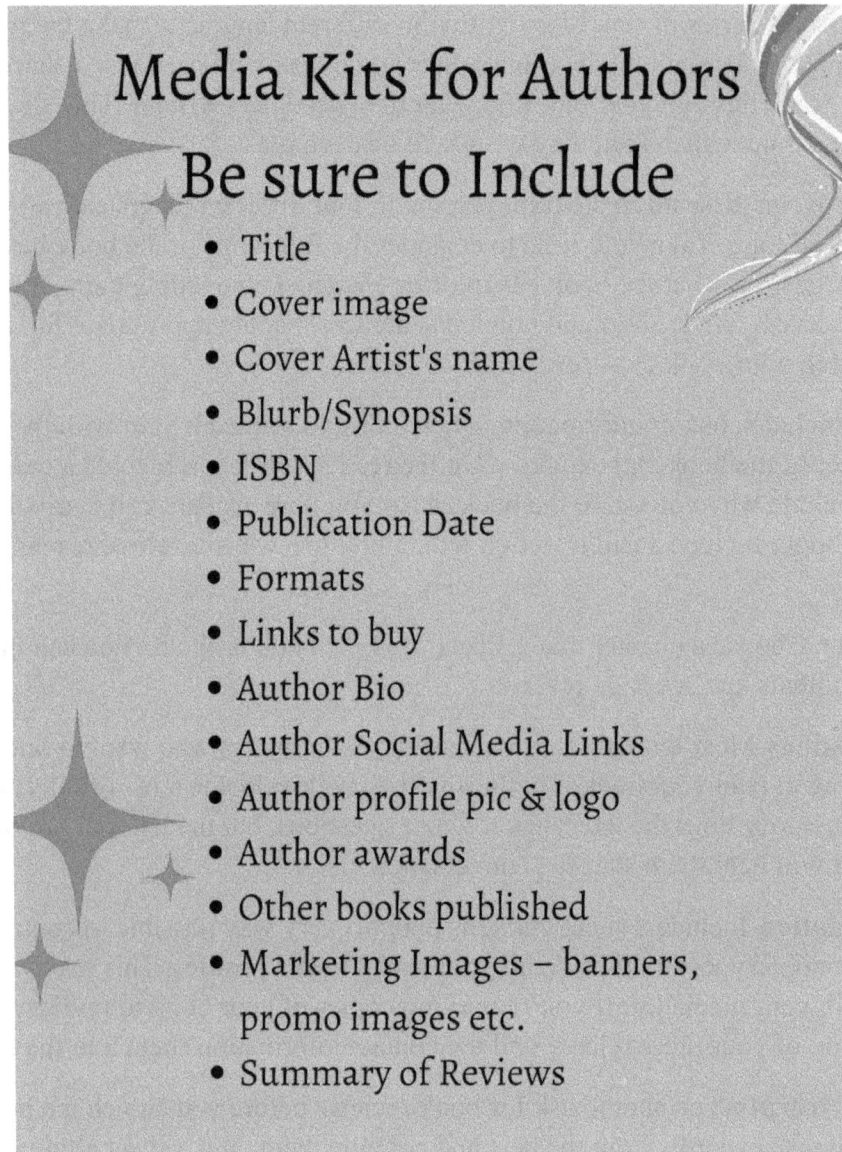

Media Kits for Authors

Be sure to Include

- Title
- Cover image
- Cover Artist's name
- Blurb/Synopsis
- ISBN
- Publication Date
- Formats
- Links to buy
- Author Bio
- Author Social Media Links
- Author profile pic & logo
- Author awards
- Other books published
- Marketing Images – banners, promo images etc.
- Summary of Reviews

Here is an example of a Press Kit made on Canva. You can set it up however you like. Be sure to include the information from above.

Jane Doe

About the Author

The media kit is a promotional public relations tool that can serve several functions, including promoting the launch of a new book. How do you distinguish yourself as an author? Why should anyone be interested? Include awards.

About the Book (Synopsis/Blurb

A media kit can be as simple as a page on a company's website or as complex as a package of information and snippets sent to selected members of the media in hopes the book will be promoted. Include cover and artist.

Statistics
Social Media
If you don't have a large following skip the numbers.

f	y	o	p
25, 256	15, 884	50, 584	10, 547

763-586-5503 · hello@bestbook.com · @janedoe

REVIEWS

REVIEW

LINKS TO REVIEWS

Where an we find this book

Interview Questions

Make it easy for interviewers and media outlets

contact details

Address

Phone / Email

Website / Social Media

The Press Release is another essential part of your Media Kit

A Press release is an official statement issued to media outlets. It is about 400-500 hundred words, and provides relevant newsworthy information presented in an easy-to-understand format. It also provides everything that the media will need to write a story about your book.

Tip-If you are ready for your press release to go out to the public write— FOR IMMEDIATE RELEASE. If you need to hold the release until a certain date, write— HOLD RELEASE UNTIL add your release date.

If you want your book to be reviewed by media outlets and bloggers, you need to send out a book announcement press release. Most traditional publishers write and distribute press releases for their authors. If you are small press or self-published, you will need to write and send your press release.

Below is a template specific to authors. Paragraphs should be three to four sentences, well written, and cohesive. Each paragraph should flow to the next. Include the 5 W's.

Contact Info   Use your colors and logo Your Name Phone number Email Address
MAIN PRESS RELEASE TITLE IN CAPS This must be catchy and grab the attention. It should be short and straight to the point and short. Headlines should include the keywords that make them easy for search engines to find and rank. They also let people know what your press release is about.
Subtitle Upper and Lower Case and Italicized This should be a complete sentence and summarize your press release
Dateline: Include the City, State, Month, Day, and Year- Introductory Paragraph- Less is more and get to the point right away. Make sure it is interesting enough to keep people reading.
Body: You can use your synopsis since it explains what your book is about. Include who, what, where, when, and why. Begin or end this section with your logline.
What Others are saying: Include reviews and quotes
Your boilerplate: About the author: Every author should have a powerful biography. Add your merits and achievements but don't make it too long.
Call to action:

The next steps. Where can readers find your book and learn more about you?

Sending out your press release: Don't send it out as an attachment or PDF. When emailing a press release, write the headline in the subject line and the rest of the release in the body of the email.

Tips for a Stellar Press Release

- Write in the third person

- Make it relevant to your readers

- Keep it brief

- Make it clear and concise

- Limit adjectives

- Get rid of jargon

- Proofread and Edit

Activity: Find three press releases for books and study them. What does each include?

Book	What does it include

- Emojispedia.com
- Smashwords
- Fussy Librarian
- Robin Reads
- Goodreads
- Bookbub
- Book Gems
- Keywords Everywhere
- Jarvis AI
- Canva
- PodcastPitches
- Clubhouse
- Display Purposes – Instagram Hashtag Generator
- In Detail Magazine
- Indie Author Magazine
- Vine Voice--https://www.amazon.com/gp/vine
- Reedsy--editors/PR for books
- Editorial reviews
- Fiverr
- EIN PRESS DISTRIBUTION
- Udemy classes for Writers
- The Artists Way by Julie Cameron
- Save the Cat by Blake Snyder
- Master Classes
- Dolly Parton's Imagination Library | USA, UK, IE, CA, AU
- LibraryBub
- Feedspot
- The #1 Marketplace for Voice Over and Audio Services | Voices | Voices
- Find podcast to pitch! Looking for podcasts to pitch? We can help connect you with hundreds of podcasts! (pitchpodcasts.com)
- Grow Your Podcast for Free | Reach Your Podcast Goals | Join Audry
- Podbooker - Podcast Guest Booking Platform
- Press Release Distribution & World Media Directory by EIN Presswire
- Press Plugs - Help a Journalist Out and Gain Small Business PR for Free
- Plan the Perfect Event - 110,000+ Bands, Entertainers, Party Pros for Hire | GigSalad
- Home ★ Podcast Brunch Club
- Advertise Your Book – Christian Book Club (ebookchristian.net)
- Top Hashtags for Instagram, Tiktok, Twitter | Hashtag generator (hashtags-generator.com)
- Resources for Emerging Speakers, Authors, and Experts (speakermatch.com)
- PodMatch | Automatic Interview Matching for Podcast Guests and HostsPodMatch | Automatic Interview Matching for Podcast Guests and Hosts
- Find a speaker | SpeakerHub

- [Speaker Directory | Recently Updated - Motivational speakers, inspirational speakers, and more! (speakermatch.com)](speakermatch.com)
- [World Conference 2022 Call for Speakers (iabc.com)](iabc.com)
- [Speaker Application – HTC 2022 – The Healing Trauma Conference (haelanhouse.org)](haelanhouse.org)
- https://app.viddyoze.com/
- [Animation Software Tool for Businesses | Vyond](Vyond)
- [Linktree | The Only Link You'll Ever Need](Linktree)
- Tryazon– Get Free Stuff
- Brandbacker - Get paid to promote brands in your blogs and website
- SpeakersHub- Like Match.com for speakers. Find gigs
- Thumbtack- Search Engine for freelancers. Great place to advertise skills as a writer and editor.
- Podmatch- Make a profile and pitch podcasts
- Show Don't Tell by Sandra Gerth

We would love to hear from you. Let us know if this manual helped you in your publishing journey.

CROWN AND COMPASS | Linktree

Nickipascarella | Linktree

https://themediacasters.com

Nicki Pascarella

AUTHOR | FOUNDER OF
MEDIA QUEENS PUBLISHING HOUSE

ABOUT

Nicki Pascarella is a prolific author of women's fiction, romance, sexy mysteries, humor, and non-fiction in the educational genre. Nicki is the co-founder and editor and chief of the Media Queens Publishing House where she curates empowering and educational literary works that inspire women. Nicki is a sought-after trainer and leader in teaching creativity and writing techniques. She unleashes the potential in new writers by inspiring them to think outside the box. When Nicki isn't writing or teaching, she finds her creative expression in belly dance.

STREET CRED:
- AUTHOR
- CO-FOUNDER AND EDITOR AND CHIEF OF MEDIA QUEENS PUBLISHING HOUSE
- CERTIFIED GROUP TRAINER AND FACILITATOR
- CO-FOUNDER OF THE BOOKCASTERS AUTHOR PLATFORM
- AWARD-WINNING BELLY DANCER
- KEYNOTE SPEAKER

WWW.NICKIPASCARELLA.COM

JULIE LOKUN

FACILITATOR OF DREAMS

ABOUT

Julie Lokun, JD amplifies the voices of those making an impact. Julie facilitates the dreams of silence breakers worldwide through innovative initiatives in social audio, podcasting, writing, and community building. Beating the odds, a learning disability, and an outsider, Julie's courageous approach to leading undervalued populations towards actualizing their fullest potential.

STREET CRED:

- **Attorney**
- **Publisher Of Media Queens Publishing House**
- **Co-Founder Of Femcasters Network**
- **Host Of Obsessed Podcast ranked 3% Globally**
- **Author of Amazon Best-Selling entrepreneurial Series Hustle Smart**
- **Co-Host Of the Femcasters Podcast**
- **Masters certified Life Coach**
- **Blogger**
- **Keynote Speaker**
- **Branding expert**
- **Advocate for victims of domestic violence**

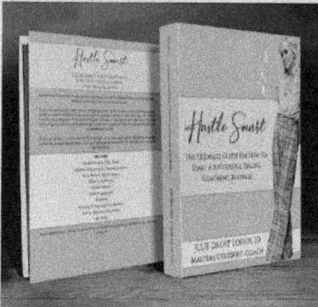

www.ingramcontent.com/pod-product-compliance
Lightning Source LLC
Chambersburg PA
CBHW081659270326
41933CB00017B/3220